INFLUENTIAL SELLING

How to Win in
Today's Selling Environment

KEN CARNES

INFLUENTIAL SELLING

How to Win in
Today's Selling Environment

CornerStone Leadership Institute
P.O. Box 764087
Dallas, TX 75376
888.789.LEAD

Printed in the United States of America
ISBN: 0-9762528-8-0

Credits
Design, art direction, and production   Melissa Monogue, Back Porch Creative, Plano, TX
info@BackPorchCreative.com

CONTENTS

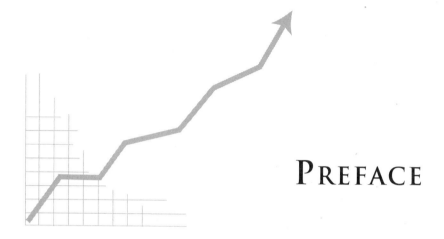

PREFACE

L ike a broken record, the questions that follow almost every
sales meeting in the world are the same, tired refrain:

- How can we generate more sales and revenue?

- Are we getting everything we need from marketing?

- How can our sales professionals improve their "hit rate"?

- How can we position our sales organization for the future?

- Why does the top 10 percent of our salespeople create 80 percent of our revenues? Why can't everyone be as successful as the top 10 percent?

In today's competitive environment, winning demands more than the old traditional sales techniques. The selling process has evolved into a complex sales **ecosystem** that stretches well beyond products and services, sales competencies, automation systems, and compensation plans.

Today's executive decision maker has little time to answer a salesperson's questions or watch a slide presentation that has a "stop me if you see something that might fit" approach. Decision makers only have time for sales professionals who can work as *partners* to confront business issues and exploit opportunities. They need **Influential Advisors.**

For the Influential Advisor, selling is no longer the timeworn asking and telling role. It has evolved into a confirmation and advisory role, turning the traditional sales effort upside down. The Influential Advisor's process reverses the priorities of traditional sales methods.

TRADITIONAL PRODUCT OR SERVICES SALE		TODAY'S INFLUENTIAL SALE
10%	Earn Credibility & Trust	40%
20%	Investigate Needs	30%
30%	Innovative Solutions	20%
40%	Negotiate & Close	10%

The following is a story about how to become an Influential Advisor. It is designed to stimulate new ways of thinking about your selling efforts and positioning them to align with today's complex selling environment. It will provide your team with new strategies and activities that will help you start winning today ... and it will change your sales perspective forever.

Read, enjoy, and then apply the principles and techniques of *Influential Selling.*

INTRODUCTION

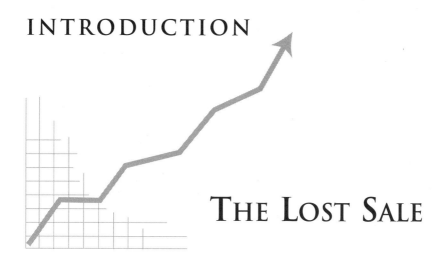

THE LOST SALE

D on Taylor, an Account Executive with Regal Electromechanical, was on the phone with Ted Spears, the Director of Manufacturing at Tardis Industries. This was an important call for Don … actually, it was a lot more important than it should have been.

The past year had been difficult for Don – a person's career shouldn't depend on one sale, yet that's what it looked like to him.

As soon as he heard Ted's voice, he had a bad feeling. "I'm sorry it took us so long to make a decision on this. It was a tough one for us," Ted said.

"I understand completely. You're replacing a big system, and no one expected you to make a decision overnight."

"That's true," Ted said. "Unfortunately, Don, you didn't get this one. We're going with Cutler Systems."

Don's breath caught in his throat and his stomach knotted. He couldn't believe it. He thought he had this one. He'd done it by the book, put out the extra effort, gave it 110 percent. Now he felt like he'd been punched in the gut.

"Don? Are you still there?"

"Yes. I'm still here. I'm sorry; I'm just a little stunned. The last time we talked it sounded like we were in the running."

"Oh, absolutely," Ted said. "Absolutely. I think you guys have the best products in the business. I know you do. I've told you that."

"So, what happened?" asked Don. "Was it the price?"

"No, you had the best price points, too."

"Our marketing material, our presentations?"

Ted sighed, "I wish I could help you out more, Don. I consider you a friend, but to tell you the truth, I don't know exactly. Remember Mike Richards, my vice president? He attended a couple of your presentations. He made the final decision.

"I was all for you guys. I really was, and he knew it. But when I asked him why, all he said was that he thought Cutler would be better for us in the long run. I think he may have a personal contact there. You know … a golf buddy or something."

Don tried to hide his disappointment, "I see."

"I'm sorry, man, but there'll be other deals. We'll work together again soon, I know it. You hang in there."

"Sure. Thanks, Ted." Don slowly replaced the phone receiver, his hand was trembling. His mind was in turmoil, "That's what it comes down to? You have the best products and the best price, but you lose because you don't play golf with the V.P.?"

He got up, went to the window, and looked out. "That couldn't be it," he thought. A vice president wouldn't give away something this important to a golf buddy, or any other kind of buddy for that matter. Especially when he knew that Ted, the guy who was going to have to use the equipment, liked another company more.

Something was missing.

Don looked down into the parking lot. Ed Newton had just pulled up and was getting out of his car – what appeared to be a new car. "Does this guy buy a new car every six months?" Don wondered.

Ed was the top salesperson at Regal. He loved selling and had turned down management positions so he could keep doing it. He was already 20 percent over his goals for the year and there were still two months left.

"How does he do it?" Don wanted to know. They were selling the same products, yet Don hadn't consistently met his goals in the two years he'd been there. What did Ed have that Don didn't?

It wasn't appearance – Ed was about 50, average height, average looks, brown hair and eyes. "Nice suit?" thought Don. He had some nice suits, too, and he'd worn them on the Tardis campaign. Don could see nothing extraordinary about Ed, except his sales record, year after year.

"It has to be the territory," Don thought. "My territory is jinxed. If I had a shot at Ed's territory, I'd be buying new cars, too."

Don needed a cup of coffee. As he walked down the corridor to the kitchen, his mind sorted through his actions of the past few months. Surely there was something he did wrong or overlooked. He'd given Tardis every product spec sheet and marketing brochure available. He'd spent weeks putting together and practicing his presentations. He'd gotten a haircut and shined his shoes before each visit.

He'd overlooked nothing.

Jason, one of the marketing employees, was putting on a new pot of coffee when Don reached the kitchen. "Hey Don, how're you doing?"

"Oh, I've been better," Don responded. "I just lost a big sale."

"Oh, man. That's too bad. I'm sorry. What happened, do you know?"

"No, I can't figure it out," said Don. "I'm starting to think it's something about the territory. I just can't get anything going out there. I'd sure like to try another one for a while … one like Ed Newton's."

Jason suddenly looked uncomfortable, but Don plunged ahead, "Newton breezes out of here every morning and breezes back in the afternoon with another sale. We're selling the same products; it's *got* to be the territory."

Jason managed an uncomfortable gesture. Don froze, then slowly turned, and found Ed Newton standing at the kitchen door.

"Ed. Good to see you. It's been a while," Don mumbled.

"Not since this morning's sales meeting," Ed replied with a grin.

Jason poured his cup of coffee and quietly disappeared.

"I'm sorry, Ed. I didn't mean anything by that last remark. I just lost the Tardis sale. I guess I was just trying to make excuses."

"I know how much you were counting on that one," said Ed sincerely. "That's a shame. I know what it feels like."

Don tried to hide it, but Ed caught his doubtful smile.

"We all have stories about big ones that got away … and believe me, I've had more than my share of those," Ed continued. He poured himself a cup of coffee and one for Don. "But you said you'd like to have my territory. I guess you don't know it, but you do have it. I had the Northwest Sector before you started here."

"No kidding?"

"Nope, and I wasn't happy about getting it when it was assigned to me. Regal hadn't had a dedicated presence there for quite a while. I felt like I was starting in a foreign country. Almost no one had heard of us, much less bought anything from us. It took a while – two years – but I finally managed to quadruple the customer base."

Don did some quick math. The Northwest had 63 accounts now. In the two years he'd been there, he'd added three. That meant Ed picked up 45 new customers in the time he'd managed to add three. "Great," he thought.

"I had no idea. That's incredible. I guess you fished it out," Don said with a wry smile.

"To be honest, I had a plan to double it again over the next two years. The territory I have now was underperforming when you were hired, so management asked me to take it on, and they gave the Northwest to you. I wasn't happy about that either," Ed chuckled and sipped his coffee.

"I'd like to see that plan of yours," Don said.

Ed laughed, "I'm afraid it would be out of date now. And it most likely wouldn't do you much good anyway; a lot of it depended on my sales technique. I think we work a little differently."

"A little? I'd say that is an understatement," Don said with a smirk.

Ed's usually easygoing smile became serious. "Listen, Don. You're a good salesman, I know you are … and I know you're struggling. The products Regal makes are a little different from what you were selling before, so maybe it *is* a problem with your approach. I don't want to intrude, but if you want, I'd be happy to go over what happened and give you my opinion, for what it's worth."

Don was surprised that Ed would be willing to help him, but he didn't hesitate, "Sure, Ed. If you have the time, I'd really appreciate it."

"No problem," Ed smiled. "I need to make a couple of calls to feel out some leads I got yesterday, but what about tomorrow morning before work? Do you have any early calls?"

"Nothing important, I'm afraid I'm back to cold calling," Don frowned.

Ed laughed, "My first sales manager used to tell me that you know you're a real salesman when you look forward to cold calls. What do you think … shall we meet in your office at 7:00?"

"That's good for me."

"Great! I'll see you then!" Ed slapped Don on the shoulder and strolled out of the kitchen.

Don took a deep breath. "Well," he thought, "if nothing else, I won't have to guess anymore about how he does it."

♦ ♦ ♦ ♦ ♦

The next morning at 7:00 a.m., Ed was as good as his word and knocking at Don's door.

"Come in, Ed. Sit down. I got us some coffee," Don gestured at a chair and a table that held a tray with a coffee service. "I really appreciate you taking the time to do this."

"It's my pleasure. Every sale is an opportunity to learn, even the unsuccessful ones … maybe *especially* the unsuccessful ones. Sometimes it helps to talk it out with someone else." Ed sat down, "Why don't you just start from the beginning?"

Don sat down and took a deep breath. "Well, I got a call late last year from Ted Spears. We'd done business before. He likes our products, and he's one of my steadiest customers. He said they had a big project in the works, and he wanted me to submit a bid on it. The next day, I drove out to Tardis to check it out.

"Ted was waiting for me when I arrived, and we went to a conference room where he had drawings and spec sheets ready for me. He explained that they wanted to consolidate what were now three separate systems into one and be able to share information between them.

He had some ideas about where he wanted to use our equipment, and I made a few suggestions for modifications that he seemed to like. The bottom line is, we were on the short list, and we had the inside track with the man who was going to be using the equipment.

"Over the next few months, I made sure to keep in touch with Ted. He was always reassuring, apologizing for the length of time they were taking to make the decision. He called a few times and asked for more information about specific products and support options …

and I went out there three more times to make formal presentations for him and his staff.

"As far as I could tell, everything always went well. Everyone I met was encouraging and friendly. I never got a feeling they were having reservations about us. To be honest, I didn't think we were up against any real competition."

Ed got up, poured himself a cup of coffee and sat down. He took a sip and stared thoughtfully at the coffee. "Do you know who got the sale?"

"Cutler Systems," Don replied.

"Did you know they were bidding on it?"

"No, I didn't," replied Don. "Ted mentioned a couple of people that he'd talked to in passing, but he never said anything about Cutler."

"Do you think it's odd that the guy you knew was on your side never mentioned what turned out to be your chief competitor?" Ed asked.

"Not after our last conversation when he gave me the bad news," said Don. "Ted said that his vice president made the decision. I got the impression from his tone that *he* may not have known about Cutler until the last minute."

"What do you know about this vice president?"

"Mike Richards? The CEO brought him on about four years ago. The CEO wants to retire and Richards is the heir apparent. He seems to be an okay guy, very straightforward, doesn't say much, and asks all the right questions. He knows his business."

"What kind of one-on-one contact did you have with him?" asked Ed.

"Not a lot. He was at all my presentations. He was always attentive, always interested. I never got the impression that he needed anymore than what I was giving him … and I never thought he might blow us off."

Ed looked at Don thoughtfully for a long moment, and then asked, "Is there anything else you can think of?"

Don thought for a moment and said, "No, nothing … except, I thought I had it covered, Ed. I really did. I was with the decision makers. I answered all their objections. I didn't take anything for granted. I was going to get this one. I just knew it. It was going to be a new beginning for me … and I can tell you, after the last couple of years, I need a new beginning."

Ed smiled sympathetically, "It's been tough, eh?"

"I've never failed like this before," replied Don. "I love sales. I thought I was a natural, that it was what I was meant to do. I guess I was just fooling myself."

"I don't think so," said Ed.

"Well, I appreciate the confidence, but I can't go on much longer like this. I'm in such a terrible mood all of the time, it's starting to affect my family. I can feel my kids and my wife pulling away from me … and the thing is, I don't blame them. Sometimes I'm so down, I don't even want to go home – just to give them more time away from my misery."

"I've been there, Don, and it's true. How you feel about your job affects your whole life – I know," Ed said.

"It really does." Don smiled ruefully, "But I can't believe you've ever felt anything like this."

"Believe it. Every salesperson has had a period where they feel like they're on the freeway in low gear and just can't shift up. Fortunately, I had a mentor who helped me out, with the provision that I pass along anything he shared, that I found valuable, to anyone who needed it."

"I need something," Don said. "Anything to get out of this rut I'm in now."

"Well, I can see you have the passion for sales, and the competitiveness," Ed reassured. "I think you're a good salesman, even a natural. And I think we can do something to help you out. But I want to emphasize the word 'we.' I can't make you a success, Don. Only you can do that. You're going to have to make some pretty profound changes in the way you look at your job. It's going to take some time, and it's going to be a lot of hard work."

"I'm busting my rear-end right now and getting nothing for my trouble!" blurted Don.

"Okay," said Ed, laughing. "Why don't we meet again in a couple of days? Is this time okay for you?"

"Sure," replied Don.

"Okay, good. In the meantime, I want you to do something: find out who the salesperson was at Cutler who beat you out of the Tardis sale. Maybe you can persuade Ted Spears to give it to you."

"I'll get it, no problem," said Don confidently.

Ed rose and put his coffee cup back on the tray. "Okay then, I'll see you in a couple of days." He started for the door, then paused, and turned back. "Oh, one more thing – this evening, I want you to get out of here on time, go home, and start making friends with your family again."

Don looked up in surprise.

"I'm not kidding," said Ed. "If you want to make good things happen, you have to start at home."

As Ed disappeared from the door, Don tapped his pen on his notepad for a few moments, and then wrote in big, capital letters: FAMILY.

CHAPTER ONE

MAGAZINES, MINNOWS, AND A BIG FISH

Two days later, at 7:00 a.m. sharp, Ed was back at Don's door, and Don was waiting – the coffee was recharged and there were oatmeal cookies. Don came around his desk and shook Ed's hand.

"Hey, Ed, good to see you. I guess you can tell I've been looking forward to this."

Ed laughed, "I've been looking forward to it as much as you I'm sure." Ed saw the cookies on the tray, "What's this? Homemade, if I'm not mistaken."

"You've got a good eye," said Don. "We made them last night – a family affair."

"Well, that sounds like a good sign," said Ed.

Don nodded, "I don't know how long it's been since we've done anything like that together. We had a great time, and I owe that one to you, Ed. Thanks."

"Well, it's going to cost you one oatmeal cookie," said Ed, picking up a cookie and taking a big bite. "Mmmm, you guys could give Sara Lee a run for her money."

Don laughed and returned to his chair. Ed sat in the guest chair munching on the cookie. He had a file folder on his lap.

"So, the family front is looking better?" asked Ed.

"I think it will. Last night, I remembered how important they are to me. I want them to have the best, but I guess if that means I can't be with them – not just physically but emotionally as well – then they're not getting my best no matter how successful I become."

Ed nodded, "Kids need their father and a wife needs her husband, but most of all you need them. Nobody cares about you more than they do. Nobody will support you more than they do, but you have to give them the chance.

"Let me share something with you. After my first five years in sales, I felt like my career had stalled out. I was angry and frustrated – my life seemed like an unsolvable riddle – the more I worked on it, the more confused I got. Then one day at work, I got served with divorce papers. I can still feel it like it was yesterday. I knew my wife was unhappy, but somehow it never registered on me that it was that bad. Fortunately, I was with the vice president of sales when it happened, not that I was thrilled about having my boss see the ugly side of my personal life, but he was a good guy, and a good manager – he became my mentor during that time.

"He got me out of the office that day and took me to his home – cancelled all his appointments. We spent the rest of the day talking about the problems I was having, what I wanted out of work and life, as well as what it would be like without my family.

"To make a long, long story short, I took a two-month leave of absence and worked things out with my wife. When I went back to work, my priorities were straight … and the happy ending? Our 25th anniversary is next year."

"Wow, I didn't know that. Seeing you since I've been here, it's hard to believe you've had those kinds of problems," said Don.

"Everybody has problems, Don," Ed reminded him. "Your success in any area of your life depends on how you choose to solve those problems. So, the family front is improving – how's the job front?"

"Actually, better … I guess just knowing that there might be hope, picked me up a little. I remembered what you said about looking forward to cold calls, so I spent yesterday and today qualifying leads. I've got two appointments early next week."

"Great!" Ed said.

"For me, it really is," Don admitted. "I see now, my attitude was probably making me radioactive."

"Don't underestimate the power of positive thinking and enthusiasm. Sometimes it's the only thing that makes you different from the competition," Ed said.

Don pointed at his pad, "I also did my homework. The salesperson who beat me out of the Tardis deal was …"

"Wait!" Ed interrupted. "Don't tell me." He placed his fingertips on his temples and pretended to summon spirits, "It's becoming clear. Yes, I have a name … Sharon Miller."

Don gaped in astonishment, "How did you know?"

"I compete with her, too, you know. She's one of the best salespeople you'll ever meet," said Ed. He opened his file folder and took out a magazine, "*Electromechanical Monthly*, do you know it?"

Don nodded, "I've seen them around the office."

"It's the major trade magazine for our industry. You need to invest in a subscription … it's well worth it." Ed handed the open magazine to Don. "This is an article about the future of integrated systems. Check out who wrote it."

"Sharon Miller," Don looked up at Ed. "She really wrote this?"

"She writes two or three articles a year for this magazine alone. There are a couple of others she regularly publishes in," Ed said. "Turn to the other marked place."

Don flipped the pages.

"Just so you don't think she's cornered the market," said Ed.

"You wrote this?" asked Don in amazement.

Ed nodded, "I know it may seem like a stretch to connect articles in a magazine with a lost sale, but there is a relationship. Let's go back to the Tardis sale. You said you thought you were dealing with the decision maker, right?"

Don nodded, "Ted Spears."

"And yet, as it turns out, he didn't make the decision, did he?"

"No, but he always did before."

"And he probably thought he would make the decision this time, too. So, what was different about this sale?"

Don thought for a moment, "Well, this time they were updating a whole system that affected multiple departments instead of buying individual pieces of equipment."

"That's right. While you were trying to pull in minnows, Sharon was landing bigger fish. I can almost guarantee she was in there working at the executive level long before this project came up. In fact, she probably initiated it … and unless Cutler makes a misstep, you won't get another sale there anytime soon, no matter how much Ted Spears likes our products."

Don looked at Ed for a long moment. "So, we write off Tardis?" he asked, making a note on his pad.

"No!" Ed objected. "We don't write off anyone, but Tardis has committed to Cutler for this sale, and it's going to be a while before they'll want to hear from anyone else. Besides, you've got some work to do before you go back in there."

Don crossed out his note, "I'm ready. Let's do it."

"You see, Don, in today's marketplace, it's not enough to be just a trusted salesperson. You have to move up a couple of steps – from trusted salesperson, to 'trusted advisor,' and finally, to what I call **'influential advisor.'**

"Let me explain," Ed said. "Businesses today are complex, and so are the systems and services they use. People like Ted Spears and Mike Richards know their own business well enough, but they'll never know our systems and services like we do.

"For example, Ted tells Mike that they need to increase output in a certain area, and to do that they need a new piece of equipment. Mike says, 'Okay,' so Ted calls you and you sell him the equipment. Everything's fine, right?"

"It should be," replied Don, "but I have a feeling you're going to say it's not."

"Well, everything *might* be fine, but just suppose that the output problem had other causes and the new equipment doesn't help. In fact, it causes other problems. What do you think Ted and Mike will do?"

"Call me to complain?" ventured Don.

"Maybe, but they might also ask for your advice. Or they might call Sharon Miller. Or they might hire a consultant to help them. They have many options, but what if, when Ted called you initially, you dug a little deeper, found the real cause of the output problem, and made a recommendation then that solved it?"

"They'd like that."

"They sure would ... and in solving their problem, you would have made the transition from trusted salesperson to trusted advisor. Can you see any advantages to being a trusted advisor rather than just a salesperson?"

Don thought a moment, "Well, the next time they had a problem that involved the kind of equipment we sell, they might call me to help them work it out."

"Exactly," said Ed. "You become something more than a salesperson to them; you are now a source of knowledge about this aspect of their business ... a part of their team.

"Now, let's take this scenario a step further. Suppose you could call Mike Richards and get a meeting with him about the five-year plan for their manufacturing division. Suppose you go to this meeting, and you don't ask him about his five-year plan, instead you present *your* five-year plan for his division, including upgrades to equipment and systems that we only have on the drawing boards now."

Don looked puzzled, "Okay ... ."

"Not only do you give him your five-year plan, you give him increased production and cash flow projections to use when he takes the plan to his board, and you even make suggestions about the best possibilities for financing the plan. What would you say to that?"

"I'd say fat chance," said Don.

"I hear you ... but what would you say if I told you that's the kind of relationship Sharon Miller probably has with Mike Richards? What would you say if I told you I have that kind of relationship with several of my accounts?"

"I'd say I need to find something else to sell. I can't even get Mike Richards on the phone," Don moaned.

"That may be true now, but over time that could change."

"How?"

"Remember when we talked about moving from trusted salesperson to trusted advisor? That wouldn't be so hard, would it? You have the products and services knowledge, right? You just need to walk in the door with a different mindset. You're not going there just to sell products, you're going in to partner with your client – to help him do his job better, to help him think about solutions he probably hasn't thought about."

"I think I could do that," said Don. "I just need to prepare differently, right?"

"Exactly ... and from there it's just one more step to becoming an influential advisor," Ed explained.

"The influential advisor doesn't just sell products and services or advise on solutions to problems and needs. The influential advisor is a valued resource for the client – a source of knowledge about products and services, and an influential source of input about the current and future effects of those products and services on every aspect of the client's own business."

"It may be one more step to you," Don said, "but it sounds like a big one to me."

"Okay," Ed admitted, "maybe you can't go out tomorrow and be an influential advisor, so let's call it a ramp, not a step."

Ed got up and went to the white board, took a marker from the tray, and wrote:

> **Influence – the ability to alter or impact thoughts, ideas, behaviors, and actions.**

Ed turned back to Don, "The goal of the influential advisor is to exert real influence on those business decisions made by the client which affect the influential advisor's own business."

"But how can you do that without being an actual employee of the client?" Don asked. "Why would they trust you that much?"

"That's a good question," Ed said. "Let's talk about that for a minute. What personal characteristics would make you trust someone like this? Me, for example. I'm sitting here telling you that you need to change the way you do your job. Why do you trust me to give you good information?"

"You've got a history of accomplishments – credibility," Don said.

"Okay," said Ed, "and what gives someone credibility?"

Don thought for a moment, "Knowledge? Experience?"

"Good," Ed replied and wrote the following formula on the white board:

Knowledge + Experience (expertise) = Credibility

Ed continued, "Okay, I've got a history of accomplishments … so what? What makes you think it's not just luck, or a good territory … and even if I really have this knowledge and experience, how do you know I won't just hand you a bag of lies?"

"Because I trust you."

"But why?"

"Because I know you. I've worked around you for two years. I've seen you help other people … and we're not competitors. We're working for the same goals."

"So, I've earned your trust?" Ed asked.

"Yes."

Ed turned to the white board again and wrote:"

Credibility + Track Record = Trust

"Okay, I've got credibility and I've earned your trust, so now you're allowing me to influence the way you do your job." Ed translated this statement into a formula:

Credibility + Trust = Influence

"That's the formula for influence – acquire enough knowledge and experience or expertise to become credible, and then build trust.

Easy, right?" Ed sat down and sipped his coffee.

Don looked doubtful, "Well … it looks easy when you put it that way, but there's still the matter of getting in the door. How do you impress executives with your credibility and build trust when they won't return your phone calls? Remember, Mike Richards didn't even listen to Ted Spears, his own guy."

"There are a lot of ways to get past that door, and we'll talk about them later," Ed promised. "But before you go into that mahogany-paneled office, you need to know what to say and how to say it.

"You had an easy time of it with Ted because you speak his language. He works with the equipment and he knows how to operate it. He'll sit there and happily talk with you all day about specifications and interfaces and software upgrades. On the other hand, we don't know where Mike Richards was before he came to Tardis, but he probably didn't come up through the ranks from manufacturing. His background could be in finance, or law, or strategic planning. The point is, you probably can't talk to him in the same way, and if you try, it'll put him in an awkward situation.

"Remember, he's supposed to be the guy in charge, so how's he going to tell you he doesn't know what you're talking about?

"If Mike needs a product review," Ed said, "he'll probably ask Ted because that's part of Ted's job. The people in the executive suite don't buy products or services – they buy ideas, thoughts, actions, and solutions that impact the entire enterprise. You have to talk about things that matter to them and talk to them in their language.

"More importantly, you need to make it quick. I know you've heard of the 'elevator speech,' the version of your pitch that you can give during an unexpected elevator ride with a potential customer. Well, every pitch you make to senior-level executives needs to be as crisp as elevator speech.

"The most important thing you can give these people is something they never have enough of – time. The best way to do this is walk through the door the first time with a working knowledge of their industry, their company, and their current situation. If you can do that, you start from square one talking about what *they* need, and you're not wasting their time trying to get what *you* need.

"Another timesaver is to present them with complete solutions," Ed went on. "They love that. Imagine buying a big-screen television, dragging it home, and finding out the power cord is only six inches long. Now you need an extension cord. So, you go out again and get one. Then you find you need an adaptor to plug in the cable. So, off you go again. You get that set up only to find that you need a new set of cables to attach it to your home theater system.

"By that time, you're ready to drag the thing back to the store, right? Well, executives are no different. They think in terms of the whole company, and they appreciate solutions that take the whole company into account."

Ed continued, "Ted Spears is concerned with equipment because the machinery and his employees are the basic elements of his area of responsibility – the manufacturing department. For Mike Richards, the manufacturing department is just *one* element of *his* area of responsibility."

Don looked up from his note taking, "So, when we sell to the executive level, we should think in terms of selling whole systems, not just pieces of equipment."

"Yes and no," replied Ed. "If, by system, you mean a bunch of machines that work together to perform a task, then no. But if you mean a complete solution that not only improves productivity in manufacturing, but has a positive impact on other areas of the company as well, then the answer is yes."

Don sat back in his chair, "That sounds a little overwhelming."

"Actually, it makes your job easier," Ed reassured him. "Yes, you have to do more work, and of a different kind, to prepare the ground for this kind of sale … but if you can do it … well, imagine making your quota for the year in one sale."

Ed's last statement grabbed Don's attention and he sat forward again.

"It can happen if you sell at the executive level and address their concerns," Ed promised. "But like I said, it takes solid preparation, a willingness to accept the challenge, and to look at selling in a different way. Are you willing to make that effort?"

"It sounds like if I want a career in sales I can't afford not to," replied Don.

"Don't get me wrong, you can have a good career without it … you just may not get the rewards you deserve." Ed looked at his watch. "Oh, man, I have to run. Why don't we meet again next Tuesday, same time?"

"That'd be great. I appreciate your doing this, Ed."

"I can't imagine a better way to spend my time. Let's meet here again, and for the next session, I want you to do a couple of things. First, go through your files and find the most difficult prospect you have – someone who really needs our products, but with whom you've never been able to get to first base. Pick a company that won't see you and won't return your calls."

Don laughed and quickly scribbled the requirement on his pad, "That describes more than one of my accounts."

Ed laughed and went to the door, "We'll get to the rest of them, but for now just the least likely. Second, think about what knowledge and expertise you have right now that could help you establish credibility with this company … and I'll see you next week."

Don stared at the empty doorframe for a moment, and then looked down at his notes. There was a lot to digest. Could he really do this?

"We'll see," he thought.

Don's Notes – 1st Tuesday

Definitions:

Trusted salesperson – a relationship in which you've established yourself with a client as a trustworthy supplier of needed products or services.

Trusted advisor – a sales relationship with a client in which you are a trustworthy supplier of needed products or services, plus knowledge and information about the aspects of the client's business that are directly affected by the products or services.

Influential advisor – a sales relationship in which you are a trusted source of products or services and knowledge about those things, plus an influential source of advice and information about the impact of your products or services on the client's entire organization.

Influence – the ability to alter or impact thoughts, ideas, behaviors, and actions.

Complete solution – a solution that not only improves productivity in one area but has a positive impact on other areas of the company as well.

Executive language – The people in the executive suite don't buy products or services – they buy ideas, thoughts, actions, and solutions that impact the entire enterprise. Talk about things that matter to them, talk to them in their language, and make it quick.

INFLUENCE FORMULAS:

Knowledge + Experience (expertise) = Credibility

Credibility + Track Record = Trust

Credibility + Trust = Influence

♦ Transform from trusted salesperson to trusted advisor to influential advisor.

♦ Leverage knowledge and experience to establish credibility, build trust, and influence thoughts, ideas, behaviors, and actions.

Don's To-Do List

✔ Identify a prospect.

✔ What knowledge and expertise do I have that will help establish my credibility?

CHAPTER TWO

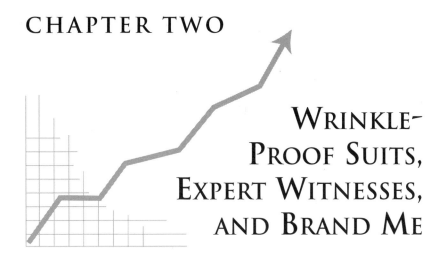

WRINKLE-PROOF SUITS, EXPERT WITNESSES, AND BRAND ME

T he following week, Don met Ed in the parking lot at 7:00 a.m. and they walked into the building together.

"How was your weekend?" asked Ed.

"Busy. I got talked into being an assistant coach on my daughter's T-ball team."

"That sounds like fun."

"It's like herding cats, but yes, it is fun. She loves it," Don said.

"Do you have a future sportswoman in the family?"

"Right now she seems to have a major swing flaw – she closes her eyes. The words 'keep your eye on the ball' mean nothing to her."

Ed laughed, "My two boys played ball right up through college. Now they just watch it on TV like their old man. My daughter, who hated any physical activity until she turned 18, now competes in triathlons. Go figure."

Ed followed Don into his office. "Did you have any thoughts on what we talked about last week?" he asked.

Don riffled through his notes, "It all looks interesting, but I'm having trouble imagining how to get from here to there."

"Don't worry, you'll understand. Like I said last time, it's not so much a great leap as a ramp up," said Ed. "Ready to get started?"

The two took their seats. "You bet," said Don.

"Okay, last time, I asked you to identify your least likely potential customer. Did you find one?"

Don leaned forward, "Yes, Tompkins-Mullins. I've heard they have equipment that should have been replaced 10 years ago, but for the past year I haven't been able to get anyone there to even return my calls. On one call, I did get routed to one of their engineers by mistake, and she talked to me for a few minutes. She told me they did need new equipment, badly, but she didn't think the company had the capital for new stuff. I don't think they're doing very well."

"That'll be a good one," said Ed.

"Good what?" asked Don.

"Target," Ed explained. "Within the next six months, you will sell them a solution to at least one or two of their problems."

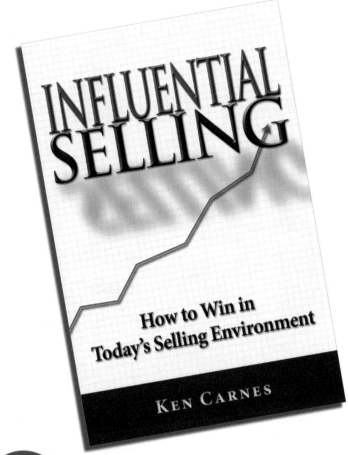

3 Easy Ways to Order Copies for Your Management Team!

1. Complete the order form on back and fax to 972-274-2884

2. Visit www.CornerStoneLeadership.com

3. Call 1-888-789-LEAD (5323)

CornerStone
Leadership Institute

You Gotta Get In The Game...Playing to Win in Business, Sports and Life provides direction on how to get into and win the game of life and business. **$14.95**

Monday Morning Customer Service takes you on a journey of eight lessons that demonstrate how to take care of customers so they keep coming back. **$14.95**

The Ant and the Elephant is a different kind of book for a different kind of leader! A great story that teaches that we must lead ourselves before we can expect to be an effective leader of others. **$12.95**

You and Your Network is profitable reading for those who want to learn how to develop healthy relationships with others. **$9.95**

136 Effective Presentation Tips provides you with inside tips from two of the best presenters in the world. **$9.95**

175 Ways to Get More Done in Less Time has 175 really good suggestions that will help you get things done faster ...and usually better. **$9.95**

12 Choices...That Lead to Your Success is about success ... how to achieve it, keep it, and enjoy it ... by making better choices. **$14.95**

David Cottrell's Newest Book!

Orchestrating Attitude: Getting the Best from Yourself and Others translates the incomprehensible into the actionable. It cuts through the clutter to deliver inspiration and application so you can orchestrate your attitude ... and your success. **$9.95**

Goal Setting for Results addresses the fundamentals of setting and achieving your goal of moving yourself and your organization from where you are, to where you want (and need) to be! **$9.95**

Becoming the Obvious Choice is a roadmap showing each employee how they can maintain their motivation, develop their hidden talents, and become the best. **$9.95**

Sales Professional Package

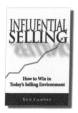

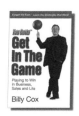

$119.95

YES! Please send me extra copies of _Influential Selling!_
1-30 copies $14.95   31-100 copies $13.95   100+ copies $12.95

Influential Selling _____ copies X _____ = $ _____

Additional Leadership Development Resources

You Gotta Get in the Game	_____ copies X $14.95	= $ _____
Monday Morning Customer Service	_____ copies X $14.95	= $ _____
The Ant and the Elephant	_____ copies X $12.95	= $ _____
You and Your Network	_____ copies X $9.95	= $ _____
136 Effective Presentation Tips	_____ copies X $9.95	= $ _____
175 Ways to Get More Done in Less Time	_____ copies X $9.95	= $ _____
12 Choices …That Lead to Your Success	_____ copies X $14.95	= $ _____
Orchestrating Attitude	_____ copies X $9.95	= $ _____
Goal Setting for Results	_____ copies X $9.95	= $ _____
Becoming the Obvious Choice	_____ copies X $9.95	= $ _____
CornerStone Sales Professional Package (Includes all 11 items listed above.)	_____ packs X $119.95	= $ _____

Shipping & Handling $ _____

Subtotal $ _____

Sales Tax (8.25% – TX Only) $ _____

Total (U.S. Dollars Only) $ _____

Shipping and Handling Charges

Total $ Amount	Up to $49	$50-$99	$100-$249	$250-$1199	$1200-$2999	$3000+
Charge	$6	$9	$16	$30	$80	$125

Name _____ Job Title _____

Organization _____ Phone _____

Shipping Address _____ Fax _____

Billing Address _____ Email _____

City _____ State _____ ZIP _____

❑ Please invoice (Orders over $200) Purchase Order Number (if applicable) _____

Charge Your Order: ❑ MasterCard   ❑ Visa   ❑ American Express

Credit Card Number _____ Exp. Date _____

Signature _____

❑ Check Enclosed (Payable to: CornerStone Leadership)

Fax 972.274.2884
Phone 888.789.5323   www.**CornerStoneLeadership**.com   **P.O. Box 764087**
Dallas, TX 75376

Don shifted uneasily in his chair, "That's a pretty high bar, Ed. They may not even be in business six months from now."

"But they *are* in business today, and who knows? You might be just what they need right now except they just don't know it yet. Trust me, before six months is up you're going to walk into their offices and present solutions to them. But to start off, you won't be selling products or solutions – you'll be selling *yourself*."

"I do that now," said Don.

"I'm talking about more than a handshake and a smile. You have to put yourself out there like you do the products. It's like creating your own brand – Brand Don."

"Brand Don?"

Ed nodded, "Remember when I said you need to do more than sell products? What else did we talk about giving them?"

Don thought a moment, "Information. Solutions. Time?"

"Right," said Ed, "but how do they know you have information they need? How do they know you can solve problems for them? How do they know you can save time for them?

"If you invented some great new thing – say a wrinkle-proof suit – how would people find out about them to buy them? You'd have to advertise, right? Well, that's what we're going to do for you, but first we have to have the wrinkle-proof suit – we have to put some substance behind Brand Don.

"Do you know what an expert witness is in a trial?" asked Ed.

"It's someone who has specialized knowledge about some part of the case that's being tried."

"Exactly. You're going to become an expert about our products and solutions and how they impact our customers," said Ed.

"I've read the spec sheets and taken all the training classes."

"That's okay for a trusted salesperson, but for the **influential advisor**, it's just the beginning. You need to know about our company, when it started, how it started, how and why we got into this business in the first place.

"You need to know how our products are developed, who does it, and the processes involved. How do you find out about the products we'll be introducing next year?" Ed asked.

"There's a kick-off meeting, and there are handouts," Don answered.

"What about five years from now? Ten years? Did you even know that we have people working that far out into the future?" asked Ed.

"No," Don admitted.

Ed nodded, "You need to find these people and look at what they're doing and understand the philosophy that drives their work."

"Philosophy?"

"They're not just pulling this stuff out of hats," Ed pointed out. "They have to work within a specific framework that includes the most likely trends and excludes the least likely trends. Otherwise, they're just running around in circles and nothing new gets developed. This development philosophy is one of the most important things that differentiates us from the competition. You need to understand our company's past *and* future, and communicate to your customers why it's important to them."

"Philosophy. Okay, got it," said Don, scribbling a note.

"This goes for the other aspects of our business as well, like service and financing. You have a target customer that's running with obsolete equipment and seems to be having financial problems. It's likely they're going to need some special programs to get them back up to competitive speed without pushing them into bankruptcy.

"What can we do about that? Are the canned service packages and finance programs we market all we have, or do we have some flexibility to work special arrangements for customers who need it?"

"But where do I get this information?" Don asked.

"It's all around you, Don. There's a company library, there's marketing material, and most important, you have 400 people in this building, from executives to finance people, scientists, engineers, marketing people … all you have to do is ask."

"Okay, I understand," said Don.

"Now the second part of this expert witness concept is becoming an expert on your customer. Knowing all about us isn't going to help much unless you can smoothly integrate us into the customer's experience.

"The only way they'll know that you have what they need is if you tell them – in a way they can understand. To do this, you need to understand Tompkins-Mullins. What's their history and their financial status? Who are their key personnel, their customers, and competitors ... everything you can get."

Don shook his head, "But where do you get that?"

"Start by looking in magazines, newspapers, and on the Internet for articles about Tompkins-Mullins," said Ed. "There'll probably be two or three corporate profiles out there somewhere. If they're a public company, there'll be annual reports and 10-K filings on the Internet. The notes in the annual reports and investor group presentations can be especially revealing. Once again, and perhaps best of all, you've got the people in this building. They're not here just to occupy space – use them to go beyond public information."

"Okay," said Don.

"The next assignment is going to be tougher. We need to start corralling all this knowledge you're going to get and package it for consumption by others. The magic words for this are 'white paper or point of view articles.'"

"Oh, no," said Don, "not writing!"

"Come on, it's not that bad." Ed took some papers out of his brief case and handed them across to Don. "Here are a couple of examples that I've done. You can see that they're not that much, three or four pages at the most. Lots of white space.

"A white paper is simply our approach or solution to a problem. It can be other things, too, like an analysis of trends in an industry, or a description of a process, or a case history, but I suggest you start with our solution to a specific problem. If you can, make it a problem that might relate to Tompkins-Mullins.

"The sales department has a file of case studies about customer problems and how we've solved them in the past. You can probably find some good information there.

"The marketing and product communications people can also help with this kind of thing," Ed continued. "In our case, they've put together packages of our corporate knowledge and expertise designed for this very purpose. You should make use of these, because they give you our corporate credibility, but I like to personalize a package with one or two items of my own because it differentiates me from all the other canned packages businesses receive.

"The next time we meet I'd like to see that you've done some fairly comprehensive research and have a good start on a white paper," Ed said. "Do you think a week will give you enough time to get going?"

"Yeah, I think so," said Don hesitantly. "I'll give it my best shot."

"Good," said Ed, rising. "One week from today, 7:00 a.m.?"

"Absolutely," said Don. "Thanks, Ed."

Ed left with a wave of his hand. Don sat scratching his head, looking at the white papers. "Brand Don," he thought. "How do you sell yourself?"

DON'S NOTES – 2ND TUESDAY

♦ Create your own brand, "Brand Me," and advertise it.

♦ Become an expert about our company. When did it start, how did it start, how and why did we get into this business?

♦ Understand our company's past and future, and communicate to your customers why it's important to them.

♦ Find out how our products or services are developed, who does it, and what their processes are.

♦ Become an expert on your customer. Find out everything you can: history, financial status, key personnel, customers, competitors, everything you can get.

Definition:

White paper – mainly, a company's approach or solution to a problem. It can also be other things, like an analysis of trends in an industry, or a description of a process, or a case history.

Don's To-Do List

✔ Research my own company.

✔ Research my target company.

✔ Start a white paper.

CHAPTER THREE

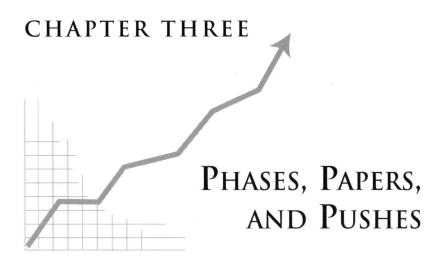

PHASES, PAPERS, AND PUSHES

The previous week had been a busy one for Don – he'd spent a lot of it finding out about his own company. Surprised at the amount of information that was available to him about his business, Don was equally amazed to find most of it just a few steps from his desk … and a little embarrassed at not having taking advantage of it before.

Scientists and engineers were more than happy to talk to him, not only about their individual projects, but about their visions for the future of the company and the industry – visions that drove their research and development.

The vice president of marketing and customer operations spent a lunch hour with him explaining their strategy for developing and maintaining customer relationships, and Don's own sales manager loaned him books and articles, and showed him the files of case histories that reported the results of every major sale they'd made in the past five years.

Waiting for Ed, Don flipped through the voluminous notes he'd taken during his research. No wonder he was having trouble making sales. He didn't know nearly as much about the products he was selling as he'd thought … not to mention the businesses to which he was trying to sell.

At 7:00 a.m. sharp, Ed appeared at the door, "Hey, Don, I hear you've been picking a few brains the past couple of weeks."

"I sure have. Everyone I talked to was happy to help out. I was kind of surprised."

"You didn't think they'd want to help you make sales?" Ed asked as he sat down.

"I wasn't sure how they'd feel, but most of them actually seemed flattered that I was asking about their work."

Ed smiled and nodded, "That's a good thing to keep in mind as you go forward, almost everyone loves to talk about their work."

Don nodded, "And like one of the engineers said, 'If you don't sell this stuff there's no reason for us to be here.'"

Ed laughed, "Yes, that's something we all need to keep in mind."

Ed held up a scroll of paper he was carrying. "I thought I'd start this time by giving you a better context for what we're trying to do. It occurred to me that a sort of roadmap might help you better understand how all this stuff you're doing will contribute to your goal of becoming an influential advisor and making a sale to Tompkins-Mullins."

Ed rose, unrolled the scroll, and pinned it to Don's bulletin board. On the banner was the following chart:

Stimulate	Investigate	Innovate	Navigate	Orchestrate	Accelerate
Demand & Credibility	Establish the Relationship	Discover Needs & Solutions	Propose, Negotiate, Close	Deliver Solutions	Maintain & Expand

STIMULATION

"In this first phase, we want to stimulate interest in Brand Don by building your credibility and creating demand for your knowledge and expertise," Ed explained. "This involves expanding your knowledge base and expertise, and projecting it to current and potential customers.

"Understand that there's going to be some overlap between each of these phases, and that's particularly true with **Stimulation**. In fact, this phase is ongoing. Beer companies spend a lot to advertise during the Super Bowl, but they continue to advertise the rest of the year, too. You need to keep improving Brand Don and stimulating interesting in it throughout your career.

INVESTIGATION

"In the **Investigation** phase, we identify an opportunity, investigate its scope, identify the decision makers, and plan a strategy for our sales campaign.

Innovation

"With **Innovation**, we begin real contact with the customer to uncover their needs and expectations. We use our knowledge and expertise to begin developing solutions for them. Then, we begin engaging the decision makers and internal influencers in our solution vision and strategy. Internal influencers are people who won't be making the actual decision, but who have significant influence on the decision makers.

Navigation

"In **Navigation**, we are fully engaged with the customer. We continue working with the decision makers and influencers to refine our solutions. At this point, we need to identify any barriers to the sale – both internal and external. This might be something like financial problems or lack of credit.

"We're also looking for potential enablers to the sale. For financial problems, these might be lease options or securing outside financing for the customer.

"Finally, of course, we craft our proposal and close the sale.

Orchestration

"**Orchestration** is our after-the-sale service. We act as a liaison for the customer, monitor progress and modifications, resolve delivery issues if they arise, and coordinate team resources on both sides of the sale. In other words, we don't just get the contract signed and disappear.

ACCELERATION

"We **Accelerate** the opportunity by maintaining our relationships with the decision makers. We review the performance of our solutions with them, identify new opportunities, and continue building our influential advisor position.

Ed looked at Don and smiled, "Any questions? Only a few hundred, right?"

"Actually, it makes sense," Don said, surprised at the roadmap's simplicity. "We get into a partnership with the customer to provide them with the greatest value we can."

"That's right," said Ed. "For example, during your campaign you may identify problems and solutions that have nothing to do with us, but in the kind of relationship you want to develop, you make the customer aware of these things as if they did affect us. If a problem is detrimental enough, it could very well affect us down the line in terms of lost sales. When the customer is operating at top speed, we succeed.

"So, I gave you some assignments last week. One was to do some internal research, and another was to begin researching your customer. Based on the roadmap, what phase do these assignments belong to?"

Don looked at the chart, "Well, the internal research is **Stimulation**, and the customer research is probably **Investigation**."

"Absolutely right. So, how did it go?" asked Ed.

"Well, like I said, the internal research here was a revelation. I'll definitely keep that going. I also think maintaining good relationships with key people within my own company can be just as valuable as my customer relationships," Don said.

"Good point. I completely agree," said Ed. "So, let's move on. What did you find on Tompkins-Mullins?"

Don flipped through his notes, "Well, I went back and found the phone number for the engineer I talked about last time. She was actually happy to talk to me.

I found out I was right when I thought they might be having financial problems. They still haven't upgraded their equipment and the competition is murdering them. They've had to cut their profit margins to almost nothing, their repair costs are out of sight, and they're still not talking to anyone about new equipment."

Ed scowled, "Did she say why?"

Don nodded, "It seems that the company was started 30 years ago by two guys, Tompkins and Mullins. Tompkins was the business guy. He handled the finances, marketing, human resources, and customer relations stuff," Don explained. "Mullins was the technical guy. He took care of everything else.

"Unfortunately, Mullins died about five years ago and it hit Tompkins pretty hard. Now he seems afraid to bring someone else in to take Mullins's place."

"Couldn't he promote from within?"

"Sure, but the engineer I talked with thinks it's a matter of trust. She said he knows so little about the manufacturing side that he might even be afraid that one of his own people will take advantage of him."

Ed nodded thoughtfully, "Anything else?"

"Most of the employees have been there a long time and there's a lot of loyalty to Tompkins, but they don't want to sink with the ship."

"Do you think there's still an opportunity there?" asked Ed.

Don thought for moment and then replied, "I think so. They've still got a few loyal customers, and there's no employee stampede for the doors, yet. This could be a big opportunity if we can do what you say we can do."

Ed smiled, "Why don't you tell me? Have you thought about a strategy?"

Don grinned, "Well, I've started working on one. I think trust is a major element here, so I need to start with the formulas for building credibility, trust, and influence you showed me in our first meeting."

"Good idea," Ed agreed. "Credibility and trust are major elements of any sale, even more so in selling to the executive suite, so you'll be working those formulas in every campaign.

"I also asked you to start a white paper. How's that going?"

Don grinned and pulled a few sheets of paper from among his notes. "Here it is," he said, proudly displaying it.

"Great!" exclaimed Ed. He took the paper from Don and looked it over.

"Writing's not my strong point," Don admitted. "So, I wasn't really thrilled about having to do it. But then I was talking to one of the scientists about maintenance issues and I suddenly realized this was probably a concern for Tompkins-Mullins. So, I came right back here and wrote about it.

"Once I knew what it was going to be about and how I could apply it to the customer, it just flowed," said Don. "I gave it to the scientist to check for me. He made a couple of changes for accuracy, but he thought it was pretty good."

Ed read the title, "Self-Diagnosing Trends in Programmable Machinery."

Don nodded, "This scientist said the biggest change in our products over the last few years has been their self-diagnosing capabilities. The machines monitor themselves and alert you to potential problems before they actually become problems. It lowers support and repair costs significantly. Then he showed me a simple formula to calculate the costs of downtime with older machinery, which I think could have a big impact in a face-to-face meeting."

"I agree. This is perfect, Don. I'm impressed." Ed leaned forward and handed the paper back to Don. "Be sure to submit this and all the white papers you write to the trade publications, they love getting well-written articles from people on the front lines.

"Also, one of the great things about white papers is that they become permanent additions to your toolbox. You can send them to all your customers and prospects. If the technology advances, you update it a little and send it out again.

"The information can also be used in other places. If you write another paper about cost benefits or employee training, you could probably incorporate parts of this one in it. You'll need a couple more, but this is a great start."

Don nodded, "I'm outlining a case study now."

"You're really diving into this," said Ed, obviously proud of his pupil.

"Well, I'm starting to see what you mean about selling the benefits of our products, not just to the manufacturing department, but the whole company. I'm finding out that our people design the equipment with benefits for the entire business in mind, so we really should be selling it that way," said Don.

"That's an important concept to grasp, it drives this whole process." Ed rubbed his hands and smiled, "All right, we've got a good start. Now we begin to really get into it. The next thing is to initiate a **push strategy**."

Don looked up, "Push strategy?"

"Yes, this is a basic part of the **Investigation** phase. We're going to push you and your experience and expertise into Tompkins-Mullins," Ed explained. You'll continue to gather your research and information, of course, but we have to start pushing inside.

"Here's how we do it. First – start collecting relevant articles you run across in the newspapers or magazines. You've got your white paper and another on the way – so think about writing other things, too, like positioning papers that define possible roles for us and our products in Tompkins's future.

"You know where the sales history files are now, so dig out some case histories that may be similar to the situation at Tompkins-Mullins and write them up.

"The idea is to create a pool of material that you can send to Mr. Tompkins and his employees. This is a good way to introduce yourself and expand your contact base. It also shows them that we not only know how to do the things they need, we've already done them!

"Second – you've got one engineer's viewpoint, but it's just her opinion. She probably doesn't have the whole story, so let's see if we can get a few more. Send your white paper (make sure it has your contact information on it!) to her and let her know that if she thinks it's valuable, she's free to distribute it to other employees.

"After she's had time to review it, give her a call and ask her opinion. During the conversation, make sure she knows that you have some good ideas for remedying the difficult situation they're in, but that you'll need help. Then see if you can get two or three more names from her, preferably in different areas of the business.

"Next, send those people your white paper or other material if you have it, and let them know you're out here and willing to work with them.

Working with Inside Contacts

"At some point, when you're comfortable with it, try to get a meeting with several representatives. Treat them to breakfast or lunch – that's why you have an expense account and people have to eat.

"Tell them that you think you can influence Mr. Tompkins to update their equipment, but you need their help to develop a plan for him.

"The main information you need to get from this meeting is their priorities. What do they need the most? What are their budgets like? What can they really afford? And you need to find out about major issues within the organization. Is there infighting? Are there communication problems?

"Granted, this is a lot to ask," Ed acknowledged, "but they'll be more likely to share this kind of information if you show them you're doing your part. Continue to use your outside sources to find out as much as you can about every aspect of the company and use it in your meetings and with your contacts.

"If you can make them feel like you know almost as much about their business as they do, and are as concerned as much as they are, they could become important allies for you later on," Ed explained.

Working without Inside Contacts

"It's best and so much easier if you can work with insiders, but if you have trouble getting their cooperation, all is not lost," said Ed, anticipating Don's thoughts. "You just have to rely more on your outside sources and do more research about their industry. Find out what the major issues all of these kinds of businesses are facing. What's their market like, who are their customers, what problems are these customers having, and what can Tompkins-Mullins do to help them? Then think about what we can do to help Tompkins help them.

"If Tompkins-Mullins is a public company, the annual report can be a valuable source of information. The shareholder letter and the market risk section can tell you a lot about their current priorities and the obstacles to achieving their goals. Their 10-K information sometimes shows specific financial details that you can use.

"And don't forget about Mr. Tompkins himself," Ed said. "He's the contact you really want to make, so begin sending your white papers and articles to him along with a note introducing yourself and telling him you thought he might be interested in the information.

"We're doing two things with this," Ed explained. "We begin educating him, and we begin positioning you as the educator."

Ed paused and took a breath. Don was still taking notes.

"I know this all probably sounds overwhelming, but it's not really that much work," Ed reassured him. "One good meeting with insiders can give you a pretty good idea of what's going on there. Later, when you actually talk with Mr. Tompkins, you can share your knowledge of their situation, and then let him fill in the details. Any questions?"

Don looked up and shook his head, "No, I understand. Introduce myself, push inside, gather information. It's pretty straightforward."

"That's it." Ed went to the white board and picked up the pen, "Here are our action items for next time." He wrote:

> **Continue Stimulation Phase.**
>
> **Develop more contacts inside T-M.**
>
> **Begin sending papers and articles to your contacts, and to Tompkins.**
>
> **Meet with insiders to gather information and gain coaches.**

Ed turned and looked at Don, "And this is very important … ." He turned back to the board and wrote:

> ### DON'T FORGET YOUR OTHER BUSINESS!

"Everything you're doing with Tompkins-Mullins can be applied to all your clients. As you develop your tools, adapt them, and use them to position yourself with all your customers and prospects.

"It's not one sale at a time anymore – we want to get to a point where you're selling all the time to everybody simultaneously," said Ed.

Don nodded thoughtfully, "That would be wonderful."

"You keep working like you have the past couple of weeks and it'll happen, trust me. Shall we meet again in another week?"

"Perfect. Thanks again, Ed."

DON'S NOTES – 3RD TUESDAY

Influential Advisor Roadmap:

Stimulate	Investigate	Innovate	Navigate	Orchestrate	Accelerate
Demand & Credibility	Establish the Relationship	Discover Needs & Solutions	Propose, Negotiate, Close	Deliver Solutions	Maintain & Expand

♦ Almost everyone loves to talk about their work.

♦ When the customer is operating at top speed, we succeed.

♦ Credibility and trust are major elements of any sale, even more so in selling to the executive suite.

♦ White papers and articles become permanent additions to your toolbox. The information can be updated as technology changes and also used in other places.

♦ Don't concentrate on one customer and forget other business – sell all the time to everybody simultaneously.

Definition:

Push strategy – pushing you and your knowledge and expertise into the customer's world.

Don's To-Do List

✔ Develop more contacts inside Tompkins-Mullins.

✔ Send papers and articles to contacts and to Tompkins.

✔ Meet with insiders to gather information and gain allies.

✔ Identify other prospects and begin the **Stimulation** phase with them.

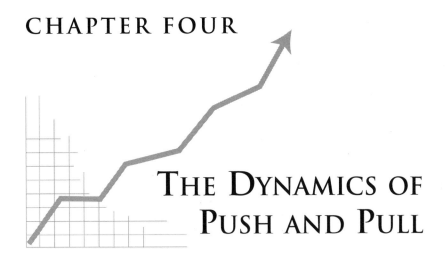

CHAPTER FOUR

THE DYNAMICS OF
PUSH AND PULL

The previous week had been another very busy one for Don. He'd sent out his white paper and some articles to Tompkins-Mullins and two other prospects he'd identified. He'd met with some people from Tompkins, and he'd done a lot more research, not just on Tompkins but on the two new prospects as well.

As Don shuffled through his notes, he was amazed at how much he had accomplished and, at the same time, hadn't needed to sacrifice his off-hours with his family. He was also surprised at his enthusiasm for the work.

Previously, preparing for and meeting with customers had caused him quite a bit of anxiety. He'd always attributed it to stage fright, but now he was beginning to think those feelings went along with his former approach. He always felt like he was going to his appointments hat in hand, pleading with the client to buy his products. Now he was starting to see that Ed's technique lifted the pressure of making the sale.

The preparation he was doing now was simply learning about the clients and finding the best way he and his company could help them achieve their goals and grow their businesses. He also thought the term "client" was really the wrong word to use. His new approach was more about meeting *people* and establishing deeper relationships than just company-client relations.

He was beginning to look forward to his customer contacts and found himself developing a real interest in the people he was working with. He was eager to move on to the next steps, and Ed didn't disappoint him – he appeared at the door, as usual, right on time.

Ed paused at the door and looked at Don. He seemed to be concentrating very hard on something.

"Hey, Don! Are you ready for me?"

Don looked up, "Oh, yeah, I was just thinking about what I've been doing for the past few weeks."

"Good things, I hope," said Ed, sitting down and making himself comfortable.

"I think so. I was also thinking how much I've been able to do and still have time for my family. We flew kites last weekend," said Don.

"At the City Park's Kite Festival? My wife and I were there. My wife loves the oriental kites. She even made one for the contest."

"We were at the other end of the park. My son, Chris, is still a little young to be comfortable with the snake and dragon kites."

"It's understandable. My wife's lion kite looked fierce enough to eat little children."

Don laughed, "Fortunately, the kites were much less intimidating where we were, and Chris loved it."

"Great! These younger years can be a trial, but trust me, you don't want to miss them. I almost made that mistake," said Ed. "So, how's the work going? Tell me what you think."

"You know, when you left last time I was trying to have a good attitude," Don confessed. "But the truth is, I was kind of disheartened thinking of everything I needed to do. It took me a couple of days to really buckle down and get to it. But the more I got into it, the more interested I got, the more I wanted to learn, and the more I enjoyed it. By the time I was ready to start contacting people, I couldn't wait. I had all kinds of ideas for them, and I really wanted to tell someone about them."

"You're enthusiasm is great, and I don't want to dampen it, Don. But I should warn you not to get too far ahead of yourself. It's easy to collect a few facts and suddenly feel like an expert, but a business has many variables. You don't want to just jump in and start telling people what they should do.

"Your discovery process is really just beginning," Ed continued. "You need to get all the way inside and see it for yourself before you start making recommendations … and you'll do that soon enough. For now, frame your ideas as possibilities. For example: 'In this case, we might be able to do this, or in that case, we might do that.' You're still positioning yourself, so do just enough to let them see that you're working on it and really want to look for solutions *with* them, not just sell equipment."

Don made a note and nodded, "I understand."

"So, tell me what's happened," said Ed.

"Well, my first engineer contact has turned out to be really helpful. She's going to be a great coach," Don began. "She was enthusiastic about the white paper and passed it on to a couple of the other engineers. She also gave me the names and phone numbers of two more people, managers in different departments, and she helped me organize a breakfast discussion with her and six others one morning before work."

"How did that work out?" asked Ed.

"Pretty good, I think. They were wary at first, like I was going to try and give them some kind of hard sell. It was like you said, they were noncommittal about my ideas, but they were more than willing to talk about their jobs and the problems they were having. They confirmed what the engineer said; they're dropping orders each quarter and having more and more maintenance problems.

"So, now I've got an idea of the places where they're having the most trouble and I'm sure we can help them, but the biggest problem is Tompkins himself. Most of the people I met with have tried to talk to him about the need to upgrade their plant, but he just seems to shrug it off."

"I wonder why," said Ed.

"No one seems to know. They're not a public company, so I couldn't get any 10-K information. One of the managers thinks Tompkins has been talking to lenders. I have a feeling they're in worse financial condition than he's letting on. Money could be a real problem."

"What do you think we can do about that?" Ed asked.

"I don't know," Don replied. "Not much, I guess."

"Don't be too quick with that," Ed cautioned. "If they still have income, which they do, they have options. Can you think of anyone here who might be able to help us with the situation?"

Don thought for a moment, "Doug Bennington?" Doug Bennington was the CFO at Regal.

Ed nodded, "It's worth a meeting to find out what he might be willing to do to help them out and make the sale. Even if you find out later that money's not the main problem, it'll still be worthwhile knowledge to have."

Don nodded and made a note.

"What else are you doing?" asked Ed.

"I made a few changes in my first white paper and submitted it to *Electromechanical Monthly*. I also cut it down to the basics and submitted it to the local newspaper. They sometimes print articles about technical trends in business."

"That's a great idea! I never thought about newspapers," said Ed.

"I'm still working on my case study," Don continued. "It's about training methods, but I've put that on the back burner for now. I talked to someone in marketing about what I was doing, and he said a positioning paper on how we fit in with Tompkins-Mullins might be more helpful right now. He gave me a general piece they already have about that industry."

Ed nodded enthusiastically, "In addition to being a model for a more specific paper, a general industry-focused positioning paper can be a good introductory tool for your mailings."

"The marketing guy also gave me some articles and other marketing material to use for introductory and informational mailings to Mr. Tompkins and the others. I've gotten a couple of good e-mails in response, but nothing from Tompkins."

"It's a little early to be concerned about getting his attention," Ed reassured him. "You'll get it soon enough."

"I did get a response from another company," said Don.

"Another company?"

"Yes, I identified two more prospects, and I started the **Investigation** phase with them. Since I was sending stuff out to Tompkins, I thought I might as well send some of it out to these guys, too. A vice president at one of the companies read my white paper and wants to meet me. I'm calling him this morning."

"Fantastic!" said Ed. "I don't want to throw a wet blanket over all this good work … discovering all this information about a client and thinking of ways you can help is interesting and compelling, but as you know, there are any number of reasons why we may not get a sale at Tompkins-Mullins, no matter how hard we work it or how good a deal we make them. It's always good to have other things in the pipeline."

"Remember who you're talking to here – the king of lost sales," said Don. "When you talked about selling to everyone simultaneously, that really struck home with me."

THOUGHT LEADERSHIP

"Let's talk about our next steps," said Ed. "We've started a push strategy in which you're pushing yourself and your expertise into the client's organization. Now we need to work on the demand side and begin a **pull strategy** in which we stimulate the demand for you. With the pull strategy, we're going to aim a little wider.

"What this means is, we don't want you begging for sales anymore. In your territory, we want you to be the go-to guy for our market category. We call this sort of person a **thought leader**."

"A thought leader? What does that mean?" asked Don.

"A thought leader is an expert on his or her own products and knows enough about the client's business to help the client plan, execute, and follow through with a strategy that fulfills the needs of the client. In other words, you don't wait for the client to tell you what he or she needs.

"That's what all this research is about. You accumulate as much knowledge as possible about the client's business, combine it with your product expertise, and presto! You're suddenly the best qualified person around to create a viable strategy to solve the client's problem."

"That would be awesome, but how do you convince the client?" asked Don.

"By simply *being* a thought leader," replied Ed. "We need to create situations in which you can demonstrate your thought leadership capabilities. These situations can be something as simple as discussions at breakfasts or luncheons, or more formal occasions, like a seminar at a hotel.

"You select the audience from your contacts and their leaders from two or three prospective customer organizations. This is another reason why you want to spend quality time developing your contacts. Your subjects will be general topics of interest to these people, but in all of them, you demonstrate and discuss *your* solutions to problems that *you* set up."

Don looked unsure, "That sounds like it might take a lot of time."

"Not as much as you might think. Your partners here in the company, in Marketing and R&D, can help you with topics and planning. It's definitely worth your while because it adds value to your sales and builds credibility." Ed stopped suddenly and looked at Don, "And what is credibility?"

Don smiled, "Knowledge plus experience and expertise."

"Exactly right and this is the perfect way to put those qualities out there and connect them to you. Last week, for example, I gave a talk about sudden, high-demand situations where a plant is overwhelmed by short deadlines and high output needs.

"I got the idea after hearing a couple of our own engineers talking about it," Ed explained. "They had actually spent a lot of time thinking about it and gave me two inspired ways of working through it.

"I set up a luncheon talk and invited people from two companies I knew that had recently struggled with the same problem. By the end of the session, they thought I was a genius, and I invited them to consult with me on any problems they might be having in any of our product areas.

"In my book, if just one of them calls me for advice, it'll be worth it. With one lunch, I've further established my credibility with these companies and developed more relationships on the inside."

Don was writing, "Okay, I'm convinced."

"And don't be afraid to invite Mr. Tompkins to your talk. He may not come, but the invitation is another point of contact, and afterward, you can send him a one-page summary of the session. If he comes, so much the better – you'll get to meet him on your turf."

Ed continued, "You need to continue implementing your push strategy, of course, but it's important for your contacts to get comfortable with seeing you in person.

"Another way to implement the pull strategy is through attendance at conferences and trade shows, and membership in associations and other alliances. If you have trouble making contacts inside a target company, these kinds of things can sometimes get you face-to-face with someone in the company who could become your first coach."

Ed took a marker and quickly sketched a chart on the white board.

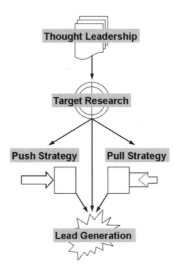

"Your thought leadership and target research combine to fuel your push and pull strategies, and it all flows back to you with a continuous flow of leads," Ed explained. "The best thing about it is that once you get it going, it keeps returning results without much extra effort."

Ed turned to Don and asked, "Any questions?"

"No," said Don. "It seems logical."

"Okay, this is what we need to do before our next meeting," Ed continued, turning back to the white board and writing.

Develop thought leadership topics.

Outline a talk or seminar demonstrating thought leadership.

Continue executing the push strategy.

He put the marker down and turned back to Don, "If it's okay with you, let's meet in another week."

Don nodded, "That'll be great!"

"Think about how you can demonstrate thought leadership with your prospects," Ed said, "and then develop some topics. Once again, like my experience with our engineers, your co-workers can often help you with this. Work on a talk or seminar and think about who you would invite, but don't forget to continue everything you're doing with the push strategy … and work on your case study – you'll be able to use it pretty quickly.

"It's a lot of work right now, I know. But trust me, it'll pay off," Ed promised. "Let me share something with you that I have taped to my laptop. I find it helpful when I'm snowed under. It says, 'There are two kinds of people – those who do the work and those who take the credit. Try to be in the first group – there's less competition there.'"

Don chuckled and nodded.

"You've done a great job so far," Ed continued. "Most of the things you're doing now, from the white papers to the contacts you're making, can be used again and again during your career. Just stay with it and keep the faith."

Don nodded, "I will. I can already see the value in everything I've been doing."

"Good," said Ed. "I'll see you in a week."

"Thanks, Ed, take care." Ed left and Don flipped through his new stack of notes. He sighed deeply. "Keep the faith," he said to himself.

Don's Notes – 4th Tuesday

♦ Accumulate as much knowledge as possible about the client's business, combine it with product expertise, and you're suddenly the best qualified person around to create a viable strategy to solve a client's problem.

♦ Create situations in which you can demonstrate your thought leadership capabilities – breakfast talks, luncheons, and seminars. Demonstrate and discuss *your* solutions to the problems that *you* set up.

♦ It's important for contacts to get comfortable with seeing you in person.

♦ You can also implement the pull strategy through attendance at conferences and trade shows, and membership in associations and other alliances.

Definitions:

Pull strategy – stimulating the demand for Brand Me so that others seek your advice.

Thought leader – an expert on his or her own products, who knows enough about the client's business to help the client plan, execute, and follow through with a strategy that fulfills the needs of the client.

Don's To-Do List

✔ Develop thought leadership topics.

✔ Outline a thought leadership talk or seminar.

✔ Continue executing the push strategy.

✔ Identify other ways to pull opportunities, i.e., trade shows, conferences, possible association memberships.

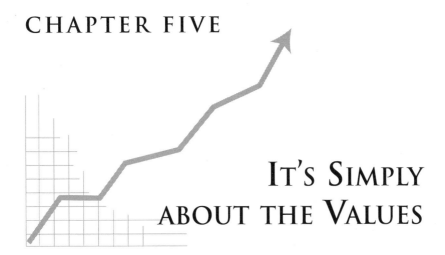

CHAPTER FIVE

IT'S SIMPLY ABOUT THE VALUES

D on pulled into the parking lot just before 7:00 a.m. Ed was right behind him. They parked in adjoining spaces and walked into the building together.

"Hey, Don, good morning," said Ed.

"Good morning, Ed. How's it going?" asked Don.

"Busy, very busy. I've got a vacation coming up soon, and I've got a couple of deals to close, and three others I need to get in shape for a backup to take over while I'm gone."

"Let me know if I can do anything to help," offered Don.

"Thanks, Don, but I think I'll be fine. And it seems to me your plate may not be full yet, but it's rapidly filling."

"That's for sure, but a plate full and even overflowing is always better than an empty one. Are you going anywhere for vacation?"

"Italy."

"Wow! That's great," said Don. "Have you been there before?"

Ed nodded, "Several times. My wife and I love it there. In fact, my wife loves it so much she wants us to look into buying a condominium this time. She has this dream of retiring on the Mediterranean."

"Doesn't everyone? But you're not planning to retire yet, are you?"

"No, no," Ed laughed. "Although my wife would love it, and if I know her, and I do, the pressure will be increasing over the next few years."

Don chuckled, "If I had the money, I'd do it now, no questions."

"What can I say," said Ed. "I love my job."

"You know what? A month ago I wouldn't have believed you, but I'm starting to see how it could be true," said Don.

"Oh, yeah?"

"I have to admit, I was skeptical of this whole thing … making all these contacts, writing papers, meeting with people … and it has been a lot of work. My brain hasn't had a workout like this in a long time. But it really seems to be working like you said it would."

Ed laughed again, "It is a lot of work, especially in the beginning. You're doing things that are new to you. It's just natural that it's going to be hard, but the good news is that it does get easier. I guess the question is, is all the work worth it to you?"

"Well, that's just it. I'm much more interested in my work now. I'm seeing my customers as real people with real problems that I can help, and I have so much more information now … information that I can see my customers need."

Ed nodded, "I'm really glad to hear you say that, Don."

They turned into Don's office and got settled.

Ed continued, "I believe that success, and I mean real success, in this business or any other, for that matter, requires a sense of urgency and a sense of personal mission. Otherwise, you're just collecting a paycheck.

"I don't care how big that check is … if you work 40-plus hours a week for all the years of your working life just to accumulate the money, what have you really done? If you can have personal satisfaction and purpose in your work, your rewards will be exponentially greater than just the monetary. And if you can make the money as well … ." Ed shrugged. "Well, enough of my preaching, tell me what you've done this past week."

"You wanted me to come up with some thought leadership topics and plan a presentation for one of them. I did that and I've already scheduled a lunch on Thursday. I sent out invitations to some people at Tompkins and my other two hot prospects."

"Fantastic!" said Ed. He pulled a PDA from his jacket and tapped on it a couple of times. "I'm free for lunch on Thursday ... do you mind if I drop by?"

"Absolutely not, you just have to promise to applaud at all the appropriate moments."

Ed laughed, "That goes without saying. What's your topic?"

"I talked to one of the scientists a couple of weeks ago and asked her what she thought was the biggest problem our customers will face in the future as they upgrade equipment. She said it was simply changing technology. Customers already have problems with it, but it will get worse."

"That's true," agreed Ed. "Computers have given us capabilities we couldn't have dreamed of 30 years ago, but they've also caused big problems. Sometimes it's difficult to make one of our new products work with older ones, even our own."

"Exactly," said Don. "The scientist told me about a couple of case studies I could look at and gave me a good briefing on what R&D has worked out over the past few years to handle the problem."

"The common base unit and replaceable modules?" asked Ed.

"Yes, it's great stuff. Customers are going to save a ton of money. Well, I figured Tompkins and a couple of others would be ripe for this kind of information."

"I think almost everybody in the industry is going to be struggling with this in the next few years," Ed said. "One tip, though, this isn't a sales presentation. Well, it is and it isn't. Thought leadership is value-added information. You're educating them about the problem and possible solutions.

"Just keep in mind that these guys aren't your actual target. You're trading good information for their help getting inside. Your real selling comes after you're in and you know what's going on."

Don nodded, "Got it."

"How many people do you have coming on Thursday?" asked Ed.

Don flipped a page in his notebook and made a quick count, "I invited 15 and they've all responded, except one."

Ed smiled, "Tompkins?"

Don smiled and nodded.

"We didn't really expect him to come, but it was good to invite him. Be sure to write up a summary and send it over to him."

Don nodded, "I've already got a two-sheet overview that I'll give out at the end of the talk. I'm planning on sending a copy of that to him."

"You're ahead of me again."

"I'm learning," said Don. "By the way, I got a letter last week from *Electromechanical Monthly*. They want to publish my white paper."

"All right!" Ed popped out of his chair and shook Don's hand.

"Congratulations, Don! You'll find that's going to be a real asset for you."

"It's already been an asset at home. My wife was totally impressed. She's going to frame the article when it comes out."

"My wife had mine bronzed," Ed deadpanned, and then burst out laughing.

Don joined his laughter, "But seriously, it makes me want to write more. I can't wait to see it in print."

"And don't forget, you can do a little rewriting and submit it somewhere else," Ed suggested. "Get as much leverage out of it as you can."

THE VALUE PROPOSITION

Ed opened his briefcase, took out a sheet of paper and handed it to Don. "This is an example of something I want you to work on for our next meeting. This is what I call a '**single-frame value proposition.**' I assume you've heard of a value proposition."

Don nodded, "It's the value we say we provide to our customers. But what does single-frame mean?"

Ed smiled, "That's my very technical term meaning that it all fits on one sheet or one presentation slide. But let's look a little closer at your definition – the value we say we provide to our customers. Specifically, what is this value you're talking about?"

Don thought a moment, "Well, it's offering the best products at the best price and a commitment to customer service plus honesty and integrity."

"Okay, now our competition, for example, Cutler Systems ... what do you suppose their value proposition is?"

Don thought again, "It's probably about the same, I guess."

"Exactly. That kind of value proposition is sort of like saying, 'We're the best.' It may be true, and it's easy to say ... but it's not very convincing when everyone is saying the same thing.

"The value proposition you need is a part of your communication toolbox," Ed continued. "Remember when we talked about executive language? This is an aspect of that.

"First, executives want to know why they should do business with you, specifically, instead of some other company waiting on hold or in the lobby. They don't want to have to dig for it, spend too much time on it, or think too much about it. They want you to tell them quickly, simply, and convincingly.

"In other words, when you finally get in to see Tompkins, your value proposition is going to be your main pitch with him, the first time and every time.

"The value proposition explains how we're going to add value to his business in a language he can understand," Ed said. "You'll work out the technical details and other specifics with his people, but with him, it will always be the big picture ... unless he asks for more."

Don picked up his pad and flipped a couple of pages, "Okay, if I understand you correctly, you want me to translate the value in our products and services into terms of the customer's business."

"More than that, actually," Ed replied. "We want to sell products, of course, but we're also selling something else."

Don looked up, "You mean 'Brand Don'?"

"That's right. You *are* Regal Electromechanical as far as your customer is concerned. Mr. Tompkins can find out from his people whether your products are worthwhile. What he really wants to know is if *you're* worth his time. That is, do you know what you're talking about? Do you have enough business knowledge to really help him? Is he going to be able to find you after he signs the contract?

"Your single-frame value proposition is the primary tool you'll use to convince him that the answer to these questions is a resounding 'yes.' Take a look at my example. What do you notice about it?"

Don looked it over, "It's balanced. It's got a nice graphical design. It describes a process to increase the customer's capacity, but it's also simple. There's not a lot of clutter."

"Right," said Ed. "You have to understand that the piece of paper is just *part* of your value proposition, and not the most important part. You're proposing to take a journey with the customer – and it is a journey. Our single-frame contains the landmarks for the journey, but *you will tell him* about all the great places in between the landmarks.

"You start with his current, not-so-bright situation, and then take him into a bright and shining future. Each step of the way, you'll show him what you'll do and what kind of improvements he can expect."

"So, it's kind of a reference map," said Don.

"Exactly. You'll put it on the table and use it to show Tompkins the way to go – *your* way. Something that works for me is to base it on the customer's basic challenges – the ones that are bringing you to him now, and some that you can anticipate his having down the road.

"Obviously, the value proposition is something that requires a pretty good knowledge of where your customer's been and where they are today," Ed continued. "To do it, you need to be well into the **Innovation** phase in which you start thinking about possible solutions. You started getting into that just last week, so that's why I've waited until now to bring it up."

"Okay, I think I'm beginning to see where all of this is going," said Don.

"So, you understand how a value proposition can be effective?"

Don nodded, "I've been wondering how I was going to handle a one-on-one meeting with a CEO, but I'm starting to see how you do it."

"Good," said Ed, as he stood and prepared to leave. "We'll talk more about meeting the CEO next week. In the meantime, continue what you're doing with Tompkins and the others, and work on your value proposition. We'll meet again next week, and I'll see you Thursday at your luncheon."

Don sighed, "Oh, yes, the luncheon. I almost forgot."

Ed laughed, "Just don't forget on Thursday."

"Not a chance," said Don.

Don's Notes – 5th Tuesday

Definitions:

Value proposition – tells how you, "Brand Me," will add value to a customer's business in executive language. Translate the value of your products and services into terms based on the customer's business.

Single-frame value proposition – a graphically presented proposition that fits on one sheet or one presentation slide.

♦ Success, real success, in any business requires a sense of urgency, a sense of personal mission.

♦ Base the value proposition on the customer's basic challenges – the ones that are bringing you to him now, and some that you can anticipate him having later.

♦ Start with the customer's current no-so-bright situation and take him into a bright, shining future.

♦ The decision maker can find out from his people whether your products are worthwhile. What he or she really wants to know is if *you're* worth the time.

Don's To-Do List

✔ Continue the push-pull strategy.

✔ Hold a luncheon and do follow-up communications.

✔ Work on a single-frame value proposition.

CHAPTER SIX

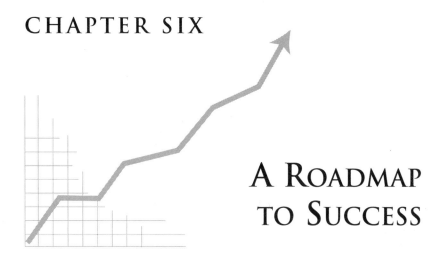

A ROADMAP
TO SUCCESS

D on was at the white board taping up a large printout of his single-frame value proposition for Tompkins-Mullins. "If Ed has any suggestions for changes, he can make them right on the printout," thought Don.

As he turned to go back to his desk, Ed appeared at the door.

"Hey, Don, good morning!"

"Good morning, Ed. Come on in."

Ed came in and took his usual chair, "I'm sorry I didn't get a chance to talk to you after your luncheon last week. You were surrounded, so I just snuck out. But I wanted to tell you, I thought it was great … a good talk with lots of good content."

"Thanks, Ed, I appreciate that," Don responded, happy with his mentor's praise. "I don't mind telling you that I had a pretty good case of stage fright beforehand, but once I got into it, the nervousness went away. All in all, it felt good."

"Well, the nervousness didn't show," Ed assured him. "I think the key to fighting a case of nerves is preparation, and I could tell you'd done your homework."

"Maybe too much. I used my wife as an audience for my practice sessions until she couldn't take it anymore. Then I used the kids until I put them to sleep."

Ed laughed, "I know a couple of families who would pay good money for that kind of service."

Don laughed and nodded, "Yeah, but it doesn't do much for the ego."

"Trust me, it was worth it. You can't spend too much time practicing your presentations and pitches. If you wear out the family," Ed suggested, "a full-length mirror will stay awake all day and give you instant feedback.

"I really liked the way you set up the problems in the two case studies and explained how we solved them. The preview of our next generation products was smooth, too, just enough to whet their appetites … and the bit about it all being top secret was a nice touch – they really seemed to eat that up. I'll have to remember that one, but how do you think it went?"

"A lot better than I thought it would," Don admitted. "There were lots of good questions and they wanted even more. I had to promise to schedule another program on the same topic."

"You see? That's how the pull strategy works," said Ed. "When you do a good job matching your audience and topic, you give them something they can see they need, and they're going to come back to you for more. It works every time."

"And there was something else I didn't think about," Don remembered. "There were three companies represented, and they talked to each other as much as they did to me. It was kind of a networking opportunity for them."

"That's a good point," said Ed. "If you invite people whose businesses or positions are complimentary, you can create a good networking environment. It's another value you can sometimes add that most people will appreciate. However, there is a danger I should have warned you about earlier – be careful with inviting people who are in competition with one another. There could be competitive feelings, disclosure worries, or past histories that could work against what you're trying to do."

"Yeah, I figured that one out myself," said Don. "But there was one thing that came up that I'm not sure how to handle. Remember I told you about a vice president at one of my other prospects who contacted me? Well, he was at the luncheon and afterward he told me his company wanted to do some upgrading.

"He said they had worked out a plan, and he wanted me to come by and take a look at it and give him some ideas about cost," Don looked worried.

"Well, that's a good thing, isn't it?"

"Yes, but it doesn't really fit in with the influential advisor concept, does it? I mean I'm supposed to be selling them *my* plan, right?"

"No, you're supposed to be selling the best plan for them," Ed explained. "It's possible they've already got a good plan. If that's the case, what really matters to you is that you're on the inside and you have a potential coach at the executive level.

"When you meet with him, instead of giving him an immediate response, you might ask some questions to get a better idea of their situation and then ask if you can bring the plan back here to look at in more detail. When you get it here, you can talk with some of the engineers about the plan and the investigation you've done.

"The chances are," Ed suggested, "we'll be able to tweak their plan a little and come up with a new idea or two. Then you can take in some other options to discuss in addition to the cost information he requested. The more you talk to insiders, the more your knowledge and expertise grows which … ." Ed pointed at Don.

"Increases credibility," Don finished.

"Right. Not every campaign is going to be like Tompkins-Mullins, and the phases may not roll out as neatly as they are on our roadmap. In this case, you'll be combining aspects of **Investigation** with **Innovation**. Just stay flexible and adapt the techniques and phases to your customer's needs."

"Okay, that makes sense," Don agreed.

"Did you have time to work on your value proposition?" asked Ed.

"Yes, I did. It's up on the board," said Don, pointing.

Ed rose and went to the board for a closer look, "Wow! That looks great."

The value proposition looked like this:

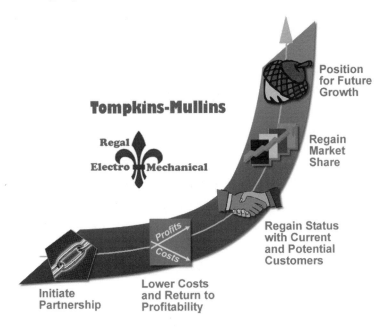

"I got one of the graphics people in marketing to jazz it up on the computer for me," Don admitted.

"It looks terrific. Tell me about it," said Ed.

"Well, when you said to think of it in terms of the customer's challenges, I thought about how to structure a thought leadership talk by setting up a couple of problems and solving them our way.

"So, I thought, 'What are the challenges Mr. Tompkins is facing now and how can we help him solve them?' The challenges I came up with are:

1) Lower costs and return to profitability,

2) Regain status with current and potential customers,

3) Regain market share, and

4) Position for future growth."

"Good," said Ed, nodding his approval.

"So, these are our steps," Don went on. "First we initiate our relationship with the sale. Then, according to some of his people, his fastest growing costs are repair, maintenance, and downtime due to equipment that's past its useful life expectancy. By replacing older equipment with our cutting-edge products, he'll see lower costs immediately. Then once we start improving his manufacturing processes … ."

"Hold on a second," Ed interrupted. "Let's talk about this cost thing for a minute. Do these people you've been talking to have access to Tompkins's books? This is a private company, so I would guess they probably don't. They're just speculating, and they may be right, but it's not a good idea to make that assumption."

"That's true," admitted Don.

"Let me suggest a softer approach, and one that can come into play at a later stage in our strategy. When you've established credibility with Mr. Tompkins, you're going to get his permission to actually go inside and work the **Innovation** and **Navigation** phases.

"You'll meet with his people and see for yourself what the real problems are. After that, you can go back to Tompkins with real solutions to real problems. Okay?"

Don nodded, "Okay."

"So, what if you made that process the foundation of your value proposition?" Ed suggested. "We'll come right into the organization, observe, talk with his people, and find places where we can make an immediate difference in his costs."

Don thought for a few moments, and then his eyes lit up, "Oh, I see. Our added value is that we can and will partner with him to lower his costs and increase his profitability."

"Exactly," Ed nodded.

Don went on, "And meeting the other challenges like regaining customer confidence and market share, and planning for future growth will, likewise, grow out of tackling them together as partners."

"Right."

"So, I guess the items on the curved part of the graphic should just be challenges that we'll work on together. But the partnership has to be there, too, I think," said Don.

Ed thought a moment, "Don't you think this whole graphic represents the partnership? If you could suggest that in some other way … ."

"Maybe I could do something with the logos," Don suggested, studying the printout closely.

"That might work," agreed Ed. "I also think it's a good idea to have your value proposition point toward a future relationship. Remember, what you're after is a long-term relationship where you can get together and discuss solutions to challenges that come up long after the initial sale."

Don nodded, "That's a good idea, too."

Don made a few notations on the printout. Later, when he made the changes, the value proposition looked like this:

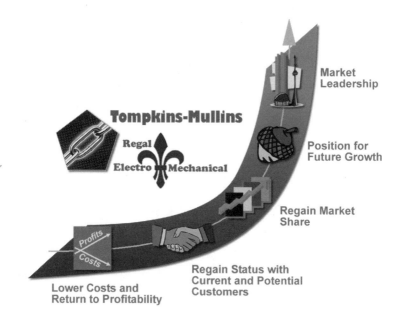

"Another good thing to do is identify some specific impact areas that will be directly affected when these problems are solved," Ed said. "You can be more speculative and general with the impact areas, because you're just giving him some good things to think about. You can put those on the other side of your single-frame."

Don later identified these impact areas and added them to the back of the value proposition:

SALES & RESULTS	PROCESS	STRATEGIC PLANNING
• Increase production to increase sales • Increase production reliability to enhance status with clients • Identify and meet changing customer needs	• Increase efficiency to increase output and lower costs • Reduce maintenance downtime and costs • Increase employee productivity	• Increase innovation to meet competition and future needs • Use current technology to implement faster response

"Then, when you take it with you to meet with Mr. Tompkins, your whole pitch will consist of explaining and discussing the contents of this single-frame," said Ed.

Don's eyes lit up again, "I like that!"

"You'll find it's a very powerful tool. It keeps you on topic and gives your customer an effective reference guide to keep."

"I can see that," said Don, smiling broadly.

"Good job on this, Don. When I first started working with value propositions, it took me quite a while to get the right combination of simplicity and coherence. You've captured it all very nicely on your first go-around.

"So, let's talk about what's next."

"I'm ready," said Don, reaching for his pad and pen.

"This time you're going to contact the decision maker one-on-one," said Ed. "Get him or his assistant or whoever it needs to be on the phone and set up a formal meeting."

"Do you have any tips for doing that?" Don asked. "He may know my name now, and he may even think of me as a thought leader – he also knows I'm a sales guy, and he hasn't been willing to meet with salespeople so far. I can't even get past his assistant."

Ed nodded, "That can be a tough obstacle to overcome. You need to find a way to get past the gatekeeper and talk to Tompkins personally. If the gatekeeper is tough, use your contacts and the communication channels you already have with him: e-mail and snail mail.

"I've gone so far as to find out from a contact where one of my targets was having lunch and then I 'just happened' to run into him. I'm not saying you should stalk him, but use your imagination – everyone is approachable in some way, and gatekeepers are often overzealous in protecting their bosses.

"When you do talk to him, here's an approach I sometimes find helpful," Ed continued. "When you're looking for a job, many job search books recommend having a meeting with an influential person in a company you're interested in before making a formal application.

"You set up the meeting as purely informational with no talk of available jobs – you're just looking for information about an industry you're interested in, and a company you've researched and found interesting. I think I've said this before, most people like to talk about their work, and for the price of a lunch, you can usually get someone to talk to you.

"If the talk turns naturally to open jobs, great, but if not, you've got a good idea of whether this is a company you want to work for. At the same time, you've possibly made a friendly contact inside.

"If you sense some resistance with Tompkins, you can do the same with him," Ed suggested. "He knows you've been writing papers and giving talks about his business, so approaching him with a purely informational meeting about his views on the industry and where he thinks it's heading is not farfetched. In fact, the meeting *should* be more about him than us."

Ed rose and went to the white board, "The goal of the call, of course, is to get the meeting, but you also want to lay the groundwork for the meeting. So, write these things down and keep them in front of you during the conversation."

Ed wrote on the white board:

> *Build credibility.*
>
> *Establish trust.*
>
> *Transfer point of view.*
>
> *Establish value: emotional and monetary.*

"You've been working on credibility and trust already, so use what you've done and build on it. Also, start trying to get your point of view across to him." Ed turned back to Don, "By the way, what *is* your point of view?"

Don thought for a moment, "Partnership for mutual benefit?"

"Exactly," said Ed, "and finally, you want him to understand that he *will* get value out of the time he spends with you."

"Okay, I can do that," said Don.

"So, what do you think about our next meeting? Can you get him on the phone in a week?" asked Ed.

"I'll talk to him, don't worry," said Don.

"I never worry," said Ed with a smile. He looked at his watch, "Speaking of meetings, I've got one in three minutes. Keep up the good work, Don. See you next week."

Don went to the value proposition on the wall and thought about how he could use it. It seemed so simple. Could it really work? "We'll see," he thought.

DON'S NOTES – 6TH TUESDAY

♦ If you invite people to your talk whose businesses or positions are complimentary, you can create a good networking environment. It's another value you can sometimes add that most people will appreciate.

♦ The value proposition keeps you on topic during your meeting and gives the customer an effective reference guide to keep.

♦ If the decision maker resists a first meeting, you can try approaching them with an informational meeting about his or her views on their industry and where they think it's heading.

♦ Work these points when setting up the first meeting:
  • Build credibility.
  • Establish trust.
  • Transfer point of view.
  • Establish value: emotional and monetary.

Don's To-Do List

✔ Revise single-frame value proposition.

✔ Begin to practice using the value proposition in the pitch.

✔ Keep it simple.

✔ Schedule a meeting with Tompkins.

CHAPTER SEVEN

ANGELS ON THE INSIDE AND MEETING STRATEGY

A t 7:00 a.m. the next Tuesday, Ed appeared at Don's door and paused, "Okay, I don't like suspense. Did you get it?"

Don looked up nonchalantly, "Get what?"

Ed came in and sat down, "The meeting. Come on … let's have it."

"Well, you know … I called not long after you left my office last week, and it was like you said about the gatekeepers. Mr. Tompkins has a good one, named Mrs. Steele. She's been his assistant from the start and she's very protective. I never got past the, 'I'll check with Mr. Tompkins and get back to you,' stage."

"Uh, oh," said Ed.

"So, I regrouped and was thinking about the 'not-stalking' method you talked about, but I decided instead to go back to my first contact – the engineer. She's always come through for me, so I thought maybe she could do it one more time.

"I called her and asked her if she had any suggestions for getting through to Tompkins without grappling with Mrs. Steele.

"She said she understood the problem, but there was one person who might be able to help – the company's controller. He was also there at the beginning, and he works pretty closely with Tompkins. She said she'd call him and ask for his help.

"Well," said Don. "She was as good as her word – the controller called me that afternoon."

"Fantastic!" Ed exclaimed.

"He was reserved, but helpful and encouraging. He said he would talk to Tompkins about it … and, well, he did … and Tompkins called," Don paused, drawing it out.

"And then … ?" Ed leaned forward expectantly.

"Oh, he seemed receptive. He knew my name from a couple of the people there, and, of course, the things I sent him. I did what you suggested and kept it purely informational at first. I told him a little of my background, and that I was interested in knowing more about his industry. I asked if he would mind talking to me about it and what he saw for its prospects now and in the future." Don paused again.

"Good! What did he say?"

"He went for it. I've got an hour with him on Friday."

Ed jumped up and shook Don's hand vigorously, "All right, Don! Way to go! This is a key point. If you can't get to the decision maker directly and convince him or her that you're worth their time, you'll have a hard road with the customer. Basically, you'd have to backtrack, give it some time, and restart your campaign later. But I knew out of the gate that you wouldn't have any problems."

"Well, I wish I'd been as confident. I was pretty down after the experience with Mrs. Steele. Don't you ever wish sometimes that just one thing would be easy?" Don moaned.

Ed laughed, "I know what you mean."

"While I had the controller on the phone, I tried to pump him for some financial information since I'm still pretty much in the dark on that. Like I said before, he was reserved, and he didn't seem real comfortable with it, but I did get a couple of tidbits – some good news and some bad news.

"The bad news is that my engineer friend was right about Tompkins being afraid to move on a new capital investment. He seems to be afraid that asking for advice from his people will make him seem weak. It's ironic because everyone there *wants* to help. He just won't let them get close enough."

"That's bad news for Tompkins, of course," said Ed, "but it can play to our advantage. What's the good news?"

"They're in better financial condition than we thought. Revenues have dropped pretty drastically, but they've been very conservative with money. They don't have a lot of capital debt and they even have a fair amount of cash."

"That's not just good, that's very good," said Ed. "If I were you, I'd be feeling pretty good about all this, considering this is your least likely prospect."

"Yeah, but finances could still be a big stumbling block. I just wish I could find out more before meeting with Mr. Tompkins."

Ed nodded, "It would be nice, but it's not always necessary. Right now you're still working on getting inside – that's the most important thing.

"When you first meet with Tompkins you won't get into financial specifics anyway. One thing you *can* do now is become familiar with the financial characteristics of the *industry*. They probably have competitors that are public, so you can see their 10-Ks ... and some Wall Street economist may have written a financial projection for the industry. If you can say something like, 'We've noticed that revenue in your industry appears to be growing at 15 percent a year,' or 'I've read that such and such product category is driving most of the revenue in the industry,' that's going to be pretty impressive to someone who may be just expecting a sales pitch."

"That's true," said Don.

"Now let's talk about what you're going to do in the meeting. How are you going to approach it?" asked Ed.

"Well, I want to respect his time, like you've said. I thought I'd tell him a little more about myself, and the company's history, and then I'd move into some industry talk. From there I'll move into where Tompkins-Mullins is in terms of the industry and suggest that it might be possible to raise its position.

"Then I'll bring out the value proposition and talk him through that. If he seems to be receptive, then I'll suggest further meetings with him and his staff to discuss the specific problems outlined in the value proposition," Don concluded.

"Okay," said Ed, nodding. "That's not bad, but let's try to outline it a little more specifically. First of all, what did you tell Tompkins the purpose of the meeting would be?"

"Getting his thoughts on the industry."

"Okay. Remember, this meeting is not about you or Regal Electromechanical," said Ed. "It's about Mr. Tompkins and Tompkins-Mullins. Period."

Ed waited for Don to finish writing, "Keeping that in mind, we can divide the meeting into four or five phases. In the first phase, do exactly what you told him you were going to do – restate the purpose of the meeting and ask him questions and his opinion about the industry.

"You can also demonstrate, through your questions, how knowledgeable you are about his business. Intelligent questions come from intelligent people. This also establishes your control of the meeting – you're the interviewer and he's the respondent," Ed pointed out.

"Once you feel you've established yourself and have an idea of what's important to him, you can move to the second phase of your meeting – transferring your point of view. Talk about your partnering concept and how it works.

"In the third phase, bring out your value proposition. Explain it quickly, get through it, and leave the sheet with him. If he wants more information about a point, he'll ask.

"The fourth phase is what you've really come for – to get his permission to come in and meet with some of his people and do some interviews and assessments. You might indicate that you don't think it's responsible to make recommendations for someone else's business without doing this kind of investigation first.

"Finally, promise to share some additional thought leadership with him and follow through with it as soon as possible after the meeting. Send him a white paper, an invitation to a seminar, an interesting article, anything to show that you do deliver on your promises. Always be looking for opportunities to establish trust, and then act on them."

Ed watched as Don finished his notes, "Any questions?"

Don looked up, "Only the big one, I guess. Can I pull it off?"

"If you think about it, Don, everything you've done for the past few weeks has been preparing you for this. Think about all the people you've talked to and all the research you've done. You actually know as much about Tompkins-Mullins as many of their employees. You're ready, Don. You've got everything you need," Ed reassured.

"Yeah, I know. It's just stage fright again."

"And what do we do about that?"

Don grinned, "Practice?"

"Practice, practice … practice," Ed repeated. "See you in a week?"

"I'll be here," said Don.

DON'S NOTES – 7TH TUESDAY

♦ The first meeting is not about you or your company. It's about the decision maker and his company.

♦ Five-Phase Meeting Plan:
  1. Ask him questions and his opinion about the industry.
  2. Transfer point of view. (Partnering concept, what is it?)
  3. Value proposition. Make it quick and leave it with him.
  4. Get permission to come in and meet with his people to do interviews and assessments.
  5. Promise additional thought leadership and follow through with it.

♦ Always be looking for opportunities to establish trust, and then act on them.

Don's To-Do List

✔ Get information about the financial drivers and benchmarks for Tompkins's industry.

✔ Practice being an advisor, not a salesperson. Connect value proposition to Tompkins's business concerns.

✔ Think about next steps.

CHAPTER EIGHT

QUEEN ANNE AND THE CEO'S LAIR

The next Tuesday, Don and Ed once again drove in at the same time and met in the parking lot.

"Hey, Don," said Ed, as they headed for the building, "It looks like you survived your first CEO encounter."

"Yeah, it wasn't bad at all. It was the gatekeeper encounter I wasn't sure I'd survive."

"The gatekeeper encounter?"

"Remember I told you about Mr. Tompkins's assistant, Mrs. Steele? Well, from her phone voice I was expecting someone about six feet tall, maybe with a whip. But she's actually this tiny little woman, about 60 years old, very elegant looking, and very nice."

"Still, she had these reading glasses and kind of looked out over the top of them at me in a way that made me think I was back in the third grade. Pleasant as she was, it was clear she thought I was a waste of Tompkins's time."

"The little ones are always feisty," said Ed, laughing.

"Anyway, I had a couple of minutes to wait, so I looked around the office trying to avoid Mrs. Steele's eyes. I suddenly realized the place is furnished with antiques, really nice ones. I know this because my wife is interested in antiques. I say 'interested' because we can't afford to buy any, but she has lots of books about them, and we sometimes drop into auctions on the weekends.

"Anyway, as I looked around, I thought I recognized the style of her writing desk, so I asked Ms. Steele if it was a genuine Queen Anne. She looked up so suddenly, I thought she was going to wrench her neck. She said that it was, indeed, authentic as were all of the furnishings in the suite.

"I told her that my wife and I went antiquing as a hobby, but we'd never seen things as nice as those. It seems she's an antique fanatic and many of the pieces in the office were her personal things, including the Queen Anne desk. She told me about how she got the desk and her plans to open an antique store after she retired.

"It turned into a real conversation. In fact, Tompkins surprised both of us when he stuck his head out of the door wondering what was going on."

"So, you have a new ally?" Ed asked.

"I don't know about that, but she was all smiles when I left."

"Well, great," said Ed, as they turned into Don's office. "Hopefully, your meeting with Tompkins was just as productive."

"It was," said Don sitting down. Ed took his usual seat.

"Tell me about it."

"Well, I did a lot of practicing – drove the family crazy again. I concentrated on keeping it informal and conversational. I did some more reading about the industry and drew up a list of questions in case we had a lull.

"I practiced different transitions from the interview into the point-of-view discussion, and I went over the value proposition speech until I had it really clear and concise – it only took two or three minutes to give a good overview," said Don.

"Isn't it amazing what you can accomplish in a short period of a time when you're sure of your words and they're the right words?" asked Ed.

"It sure helps avoid fumbling and lapses of memory," Don agreed. "I also had a couple of case histories I thought were relevant that I could talk about, so I was confident when I went in.

"Tompkins is really a great guy, very cordial. The entire meeting was very comfortable, so I started in on the first phase, talking about his industry and how things have changed since he started. I don't think I fooled him about my real purpose in being there, but he answered my questions and talked freely. I learned a few more things about the industry in general that I'm sure I'll be able to use with other customers.

"And you were right about asking intelligent questions. I asked him what he thought about the current trend of customers asking for more and more individual customization. He was surprised that I knew about that, and as it turns out, it's an issue that concerns him."

"Did you get an idea of the man himself and what's important to him?" asked Ed.

"Yes, I think I did. He was surprisingly frank about what's happened over the past few years. He and Mullins were roommates in college – Mullins got a degree in engineering and Tompkins got his in business – so after graduation they decided to pool their abilities and start this company.

"It's what we thought. Tompkins handled all the front office responsibilities, and Mullins did all the manufacturing and shipping work. It was a good arrangement until Mullins died. Unfortunately, they had never bothered to learn much about each others' jobs, so Tompkins was very uncomfortable having to make decisions for the other side of the business. Plus, he didn't really know the personnel there very well.

"He admitted he didn't know who he could trust and said he tried to get to know them better, but the technical language was a barrier, so he wasn't comfortable asking a lot of questions.

"I was sympathetic," Don said, "and told him a couple of my own stories about the technical language problem."

"Good job," said Ed.

"The bottom line is that he's most concerned about just keeping the business going and keeping his employees working. He knows what the numbers mean.

"There was a point in talking about his staff when it felt like a good time to move to phase two, the point of view.

"I told him that we are a company with good people, too, and our policy is to use all of them. Not just to manufacture products but to help our customers become and stay successful. We have people who can understand the problems and work with his team to make the issues understandable to him."

"Good transition," said Ed.

"I told him about a case history in which we sent a couple of engineers to the customer's site, and how they studied the entire process, not just the equipment. When they were done, the engineers recommended adjustments to our machine *and* some of the older equipment that wasn't ours. Then they stayed until the adjustments were made and everything was working to the customer's satisfaction.

"Then I pulled out the value proposition and explained how we would work with him and his people to make improvements. I emphasized that we could focus on the different stages shown in the diagram: First, returning to profitability, then when that was accomplished, regaining customer confidence and market share. After that, if they were still happy with the arrangement, we could start looking toward future requirements and innovations targeted at making them market leaders.

"He seemed to like the single-frame a lot," Don concluded. "Anyway, I offered to meet with some of his people, bring in some of our experts, work with them to study his processes, and develop a starting plan that would work and they could afford. Once completed, he could use the information anyway he wanted."

"Did he go for that?"

"How could he refuse? He called in Mrs. Steele and asked her to help me set up the appointments."

"Fantastic! You're a pro already."

"It was very natural, Ed. The **Investigation** and **Innovation** work was hard, but it was worth it. I really felt like I already knew this guy," said Don.

"I also proposed that we meet after the study so I could present our results to him privately. He went for that, too.

"Oh, and thought leadership … a point came up about customer deadlines. I told him we just happened to have some good information on that and I'd be sure to send it along to him, so I sent him your paper about high-demand and quick deadlines."

"I get royalties, you know," said Ed, grinning.

Don grinned back, "Oh, can you put that on my tab?"

"Just make this sale and we'll be square," said Ed. "Now you move into the **Navigation** stage. You're inside, so make the most of it. Look at everything you can and identify as many barriers and enablers to the sale as possible. Do you know who you're going to take with you from here?"

Don nodded, "There are two engineers I've been consulting with on this all along. They're very experienced and seem to have a good idea of what's going on there already. They've agreed to take a couple of field trips and committed to work with me on it."

"Great, and don't forget, if you run into any stumbling blocks, you've got a building full of other people who'll be happy to help you get over them."

"Don't worry, I'm counting on that."

"They ... *we* won't let you down," Ed assured. "Well, Don, it looks to me like everything is under control and cruising along. Do you have any questions or is there anything I can help you with now?"

"No ... right now I'm pretty comfortable with what I need to do, but keep your phone with you."

"24-7," said Ed with a smile. "Next week, same time, same place?"

"You bet."

DON'S NOTES – 8TH TUESDAY

♦ Once inside, look at everything you can and identify as many barriers and enablers to the sale as possible.

♦ Don't talk – listen.

♦ Gatekeepers play an important role. They let people who bring value in and keep time-wasters out. Always bring value.

Don's To-Do List

✓ Coordinate and facilitate meetings with insiders.

✓ Schedule and facilitate on-site visits with our engineers.

✓ Continue expanding knowledge of the customer from the inside and build the influential advisor position.

CHAPTER NINE

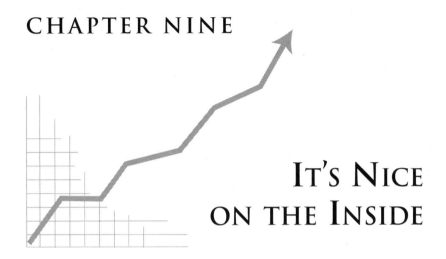

IT'S NICE
ON THE INSIDE

E d stepped into Don's office at the usual time and stopped.

Don was on the phone but waved him in. It soon became apparent to Ed that Don was talking to one of his Tompkins-Mullins contacts. He'd sent her an invitation to a luncheon seminar and she was calling to ask if she could invite a colleague from another company.

After a couple of minutes, Don hung up and Ed grinned at him, "It sounds like your fan base is growing."

Don laughed, "I don't know if you can call them fans, but it is amazing how much enthusiasm I'm getting for my push-pull and thought leadership pieces. People really seem to need information and they don't have a lot of time to dig through all of the sources available to find relevant material."

"That's true," said Ed. "I found that after a while you don't even have to come up with subject matter – your audiences will begin telling you what they need."

Don nodded, "I've already had a couple of people suggest topics."

"One tip, though – if you do plan a talk on a suggested topic, call the person who suggested it and encourage him or her to invite two or three other people. I've expanded my contact base by doing that."

"That's a good idea," said Don, making a note.

"How's your **Navigation** at Tompkins-Mullins going?" Ed asked.

"I've had two meetings with two different groups of people there," Don began. "My engineering team gave me a list of points to discuss and asked for some specific information they thought they would need. After that, I took the engineers inside to look at the plant and talk to a couple of their people. The first two meetings helped the engineers maximize the use of their time.

"Everyone got along well, and we all agreed on what's needed to get things back up to speed. There's one machine that's costing them a ton of money in terms of downtime and repairs. Plus, even when it is working, it's a bottleneck due to low capacity. So, we definitely want to do something about that.

"There are two other machines that aren't quite as bad, but they are well past their prime. If we could replace those, too, it would get manufacturing back to an output capability they could live with for a while."

"So, it doesn't look like they're going to have to bankrupt themselves to get back into the game?" asked Ed.

"Not even close," said Don. "Still, I'm going to meet with our CFO and see if I can get two or three financing options for them."

"Great!" said Ed. "So, let's review. You have a realistic solution to which they've contributed and that they can afford, and you're working on financing options. The next step is to fulfill your promise to Mr. Tompkins and meet with him about the results of your review.

"When you meet with him, once again, be careful how you phrase things. Remember, even though you've had a meeting of minds with his team, you're still not yet partners. And you won't be until Mr. Tompkins signs our contract.

"Continue to use your CEO language – he doesn't want to hear the details of unplugging the old machines and plugging in the new ones. He wants to know what effect these changes will have on his business in terms of customer goodwill and profitability," Ed advised.

"You might even want to put together a map for him that you can explain, like your value proposition. Something like, 'This is the manufacturing line. Here's where we have this problem, and this is where we have these problems, and that's where the new equipment will go.' Make the actual recommendations in bullet points and don't go into a lot of detail unless he asks. And, as much as possible, stress the great cooperation and team effort everyone gave in coming up with these recommendations. Let him know, you're old friends now working together on a mutual problem.

"When you feel like you've given him all the information he needs and he understands it, ask for permission to come back and present a formal proposal with pricing and scope. If things go as well as they have been, this should be an easy okay.

"Have you set a date for your next meeting with him?" asked Ed.

"This week … on Thursday."

"Good. What about your other business? How's that going?"

"I've got two more potentials involved in, or targeted for push-pull, one I'm starting **Navigation** with and another I'll get into **Navigation** with next week. One of the newer contacts read my white paper in *Electromechanical Monthly*, he knew my name."

"You see? Free advertising for Brand Don," Ed emphasized. "What do you think now, was writing the white paper worth your time?"

"Absolutely. This guy was impressed. It was instant credibility," said Don.

"Exactly. Good job," said Ed, rising to leave. "Well, I'll let you get to it, but you're doing great, Don. I'm proud of you. You're going to get this sale, I can feel it. I'll see you next week."

After Ed left, Don smiled and thought, "I'm getting more than this one, Ed. Next year at this time, you just may be number two."

DON'S NOTES – 9TH TUESDAY

- ♦ People don't have a lot of time to dig through all of the sources available to find information relevant to them. After a while, your seminar audiences will tell you what they need.

- ♦ When reviewing the results of your **Navigation** study with the decision maker, make your recommendations in bullet points – don't go into a lot of detail unless they ask for it. Keep it consultative.

- ♦ Deliver your message to the decision maker crisply and from an advisor's stance.

- ♦ Stress the great cooperation and team effort everyone gave in coming up with the recommendations.

- ♦ Thought leadership is free advertising for Brand Me and your organization.

Don's To-Do List

✔ Make a map that graphically shows proposed changes.

✔ Practice the review, and practice some more.

✔ Ask Tompkins for permission to come back and present a formal proposal with pricing and scope.

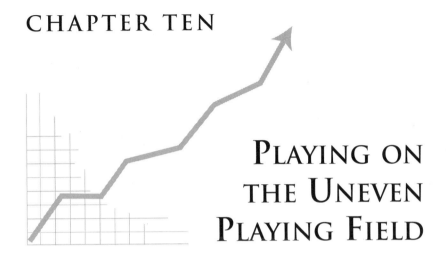

CHAPTER TEN

PLAYING ON THE UNEVEN PLAYING FIELD

The next Tuesday, Don sat at his desk working on his formal proposal for the Tompkins-Mullins sale, and even though it was only just before 7:00 a.m., he'd been there for over two hours.

It seemed like there were a million details that needed to be included in the proposal: shipping and installation costs, insurance, service agreements, warranties, spare parts, and on and on. Every little detail had to be checked and double-checked, both to protect Regal from costly mistakes and to insure that he was putting together the best deal possible.

The second meeting with Tompkins had gone well … very well. They were more relaxed with each other and worked together like they'd been doing it for years. Putting the elements of the recommendations into a language Tompkins could connect with hadn't been easy, but it had been worth it. He had been very receptive and asked few questions. It was obvious that he had been talking more with his people.

Then Don asked if he could put together a formal proposal, and Tompkins dropped the other shoe. Of course Don could present a formal proposal, but Tompkins was also asking for proposals from other vendors, based on Regal's recommendations.

For the first time in his meetings with Tompkins, Don was pulled up short. He fumbled past it, hoping that he didn't look too surprised. He didn't know why he hadn't foreseen this.

Of course they were going to request other proposals, so why hadn't he thought about that? It was déjà vu. He was back at square one, waiting for the results of a sales effort that could make or break his career.

When Ed appeared at the door, Don was still lost in thought. "Hey there, Mr. Taylor, are you awake?"

Don looked up suddenly, "Oh, yeah, come in, Ed. I've been here a while."

Ed looked at him more closely as he sat down, "A long while?" he asked.

"Quite a while," said Don. "The meeting with Tompkins didn't … well, it didn't go quite as I anticipated."

"He wants to see a proposal, doesn't he?" asked Ed.

"Oh, yeah, no problem with that. In fact, he wants to see several – from other vendors."

"Oh? A little competition? You're not going to let a little thing like that get you down, are you?"

"No, no, I'm not down. I guess I just got used to having these guys all to myself. I'm a little concerned about having done all this work for nothing," said Don.

"For nothing? If you lose this sale, you think you've done all this for nothing? Come on, Don, you've got more sense than that. You've got prospects in the pipeline. You've got a foundation for a whole new career. Tompkins-Mullins is just a small, troubled company. In terms of what you'll accomplish over the next few years, it's a grain of sand on the beach … and besides, what makes you think you're going to lose it?"

"I just keep thinking of Sharon Miller having a one-on-one with Tompkins," said Don. "I can't seem to shake the frustration I had with the Tardis loss."

"Let's think about that loss for a minute, Don. There are some similarities, but there's also one really big difference. What is it?" Ed asked.

Don thought for a few seconds, "Our positions are reversed?"

Ed nodded, smiling, "Exactly. You're inside and she's outside. You know all the players and she knows no one. Cutler Systems may or not get a request for a proposal, and if they do, Sharon may or may not be their rep. But if she is, you should be enjoying your position, not worrying about it."

"You're right," Don agreed. "It's just hard for me to realize that. For once, I have the advantage on a sale."

"Get used to it, it won't be the last time," said Ed.

"I'll try," promised Don.

"Now that we've gotten that out of the way, tell me about your meeting."

"Well, except for that, it was great," Don said, beginning to relax. "It all went according to plan. I translated everything into CEO language and related each challenge to its impact on revenue, the possible cost savings from our remedies, and intangibles like employee morale and customer goodwill.

"I made a map of his manufacturing floor, like you said, and explained to him where we thought the three most-needed changes were. At each of the three points, I gave him a breakdown of his current costs, approximate costs for the replacement, approximate ongoing costs, and approximate return on investment.

"I also used the value proposition to show him what progress this was going to buy us and suggested what next steps we might take to move on from there."

"How did he respond?" asked Ed.

"He was a very active participant. He understood it all and asked lots of good questions. The only place where he had reservations was in the startup costs. He's fiscally very conservative, and admittedly, it could drain lot of his cash and not leave him with many options if these things don't give the results we think they will.

"I told him I would talk to our finance people and come up with some options that would minimize his upfront expense and give him some breathing room," Don continued. "I tried to make it clear that it's not to our advantage to sell him three pieces of equipment and then sit back and watch him fail. I made a personal commitment to him to do everything I could to make sure all of the good things we'd been talking about actually happened."

"Good. Personal commitment is an inexpensive thing for us to offer, but if you follow through on it, it's priceless in terms of trust and credibility. When do you think you'll pitch the proposal?" Ed asked.

"This week. I have an appointment on Friday," said Don.

"Okay, there's not much advice I can give you at this point," said Ed. "You know how to work up a proposal. Just make sure it covers everything you talked about and that it's accurate. Double-check everything in it. Catching a mistake before the pitch can save you giant headaches and giant customer dissatisfaction, not to mention a lot of money for the company.

"As far as preparing your presentation, I'll tell you how I organize mine and you can use it or not. You know a lot better than I do what will work best for these guys."

Ed went to the white board and wrote:

Present and confirm current state.

"First, I like to summarize the current state of the customer's business based on everything I've seen and heard, and confirm that everyone sees it the same way."

Ed turned and wrote:

Present and confirm future state.

"This is like the current-state talk, but you present your vision of the business after the sale when everything is up and running. I always like to do a little extra and really try to create a picture of what it's going to be like, and how wonderful it's going to be for them when the changes are in place. Like, no more having to shut down the assembly line for two hours only to find that the old machine stopped because a janitor swept away the matchbook that was holding it level. Once again, get confirmation that this is his understanding of what's supposed to happen."

Ed wrote again:

Present a bridge between these two states (the proposal).

"Present the proposal as being a bridge from the old misery to the new paradise. Obviously, there will be details to be explained, but try to keep it an overview as much as possible," Ed explained. "The proposal is a discussion document, not a contract, so limit your long-winded speeches to items he specifically requests more information about.

"Don't leave until you're sure he understands everything you've talked about and that you've answered every last one of his questions."

Ed went back to his chair. "Any questions?" he asked.

Don shook his head, "No, that structure makes sense – it sort of reflects the whole process we've just worked through."

Ed sighed a deep breath and smiled, "Well, we've come a long way and we're finally heading into the finish. You've done really well, Don. I can't imagine a better or more conscientious student.

"There's no sense in meeting until after you've gotten the decision, so why don't you give me a call then and we'll arrange a last meeting."

"That sounds like a plan," said Don.

Ed rose and started for the door, "This is going to be a win, Don. I've got that feeling I always get before I get a sale, but I don't have one on the line right now so it must be yours."

"Thanks, Ed, I'll talk to you later."

Don sat back in his chair and took a deep breath. "A win," he thought. "Definitely, a win."

DON'S NOTES – 10TH TUESDAY

♦ Once established, the position of influential advisor is almost impossible to compete against.

♦ Personal commitment is an inexpensive thing to offer, but if you follow through on it, it's priceless in terms of trust and credibility.

♦ Double-check everything in the proposal. Catching a mistake before the pitch can save you giant headaches and giant customer dissatisfaction, not to mention a lot of money for the company.

♦ In the proposal presentation:
  • Present and confirm current state.
  • Present and confirm future state.
  • Present a bridge between these two states (the proposal).

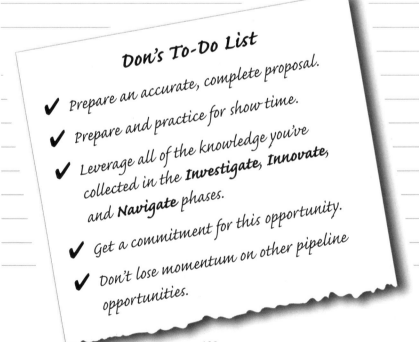

Don's To-Do List

✔ Prepare an accurate, complete proposal.

✔ Prepare and practice for show-time.

✔ Leverage all of the knowledge you've collected in the **Investigate, Innovate,** and **Navigate** phases.

✔ Get a commitment for this opportunity.

✔ Don't lose momentum on other pipeline opportunities.

CHAPTER ELEVEN

IN THE FERTILE
FIELDS OF SUCCESS

It was the final Tuesday, just before 7:00 a.m.

The previous Friday, Ray Tompkins had called Don to give him the news – he was accepting the Regal proposal.

Don had shut his door, sent his calls to voice mail, and spent the next hour leaning back in his chair and breathing freely for the first time in many months.

That weekend he had taken his wife and kids out for a long, afternoon picnic. Relaxing on a blanket and watching his family at play, he felt like a new life full of exciting possibilities was beginning to unroll before them.

He heard a noise and looked up. Ed was standing at the door, knocking on the doorframe. "Am I interrupting some deep thinking?"

"Come in, Ed," Don said. "No, not that deep. I was just thinking how different I feel today from that first Tuesday we got together."

"Hopefully, that's a good thing."

"Oh, yeah."

"Well, congratulations, Don. Good job. Good sale." Ed stepped up to the desk and shook Don's hand. "How do you think the proposal presentation went?"

"Smooth as glass, Ed. I did just what you suggested – current business state, future business state, bridge between the two. It was very natural … and they loved it."

"You painted a pretty picture of the future for them?" Ed asked.

"Oz didn't look this good to Dorothy."

Ed laughed, "As long as you can make it happen for them."

"I didn't overreach," Don assured his mentor. "I'll give them their money's worth and a lot more, I promise."

"You said *they* loved it. It wasn't just Tompkins?"

"No, there was his accountant, the controller, and a senior engineer at the table," Don said. "I thought the engineer was a really good sign. Tompkins deferred to him a couple of times and asked him a few questions. It looks like he's finally opened a communications channel to the manufacturing side."

Ed smiled, "Maybe we should bill them for management consulting services."

"There were times during this campaign when I thought that might not be a bad idea," laughed Don. "The accountant was really impressed that I had come with four different financing and lease-to-own options. He asked me all kinds of questions I couldn't answer – after the meeting, fortunately.

"I'm going to get together with him and our CFO and nail down the financial stuff before we negotiate the actual contract."

"Fantastic. How are you doing with your other business?" asked Ed.

"Really well," Don replied. "I'm presenting another formal proposal next week. That situation is completely different. The customer is in a rapid growth phase, and they were so impressed with our inside consulting during **Navigation** that they proposed contracting with us to do that for the next couple of years.

"I talked with our vice president of engineering and he liked the idea, so we worked out a couple of preliminary plans to take back to them," Don continued. "If it works out with these guys, we might begin offering these kinds of services as regular products."

"No kidding," said Ed. "Good job in following through with that."

"Before you came along," said Don, "even if a customer had asked about that kind of thing, I would have just said, 'No, we don't do that.' You've opened my eyes to a whole new world of possibilities."

"I think it's more of a sign that you're enjoying what you're doing," Ed countered. "That kind of creative thinking requires a receptive frame of mind."

Don fell silent for a moment, "Well, I can't believe it's our last meeting. I can't help thinking that there's a lot more I need to know."

"There are a couple of phases left in the process: **Orchestration** and **Acceleration**. I'll talk generally about those today, but they're really separate topics on their own. When I get back from vacation we can do another series on those subjects if you're interested."

"Definitely, but I'd also appreciate anything you can give me now," said Don.

"Okay, at this point you're like a farmer who's cleared a new field, plowed, sown, and just taken his first harvest from it. So, what does a farmer do?"

"I'm afraid I'm a city boy," Don said with a shrug.

"The farmer prepares the field for another plowing, planting, and harvest cycle. Once you have a field that's producing for you and has the potential for many more harvests, are you just going to abandon it?"

"I guess not," said Don.

"We're getting into something I call **harvest strategies**, and there are many ways to keep a field fertile over time, but the first and best is to make sure Tompkins gets exactly what you've promised them. I call that **Orchestrating** the sale.

"You take charge and make sure the product gets built, tested, shipped, installed, and running just the way you said it would. It's your responsibility to get your harvest to the market – no one else will care as much as you.

"Most salespeople get the contract signed, put in the order, and then, unless the customer calls them, it's history. But you've got more at stake here than an order."

"Brand Don," said Don.

"Exactly. You've worked hard the past several weeks to build your brand and it's paying off for you, but one ignored phone call can destroy it.

"Remember the influential advisor is a lot more than a salesperson – your responsibilities are greater and your rewards are proportionally greater. But the rewards won't come if you don't follow through on the responsibilities.

"Your customers should feel as though you actually work for them, and you should have that same feeling. You should project to your customers the same conscientiousness you apply to Regal.

"**Acceleration** comes after the sale is complete and is really just doing more of what you've been doing," Ed explained. "You've told these people you wanted to partner with them, and most people rank business partners just below family in importance. Even the most ungrateful children phone their mothers on Mother's Day. Bottom line, stay connected to your contacts.

"One of the most important aspects of **Acceleration** is to check back in and review the performance of your solutions and listen for other opportunities to help. Are they working the way you said they would? Have they enhanced performance? You can claim to care about providing real solutions all you want, but if you don't check on how they worked out, the claim will be hollow.

"Well," concluded Ed, "that's about it – **Orchestration** and **Acceleration** – two areas most salespeople miss. Any questions?"

"Not right now, but I'm sure I will."

Ed smiled and stood up, "I'm right down the hall if you ever need to talk."

Don rose and shook Ed's hand. "Thanks, Ed, I appreciate that, and if I can do anything for you, you know I owe you ... big time."

"The truth is, Don, the feeling I get from seeing someone else succeed using my methods is almost as good as landing a big sale. Thank *you* for the opportunity."

Don's Notes – 11th Tuesday

♦ Once you have a field that's producing for you and has the potential for many more harvests, don't abandon it.

♦ The first and best way to keep a field fertile over time is to make sure the customer gets exactly what you've promised them.

♦ Leverage the results you've achieved to gain additional business.

♦ The **Influential Advisor** is a lot more than a salesperson – the responsibilities are greater and the rewards are proportionally greater. But the rewards won't come if you don't follow through on the responsibilities.

Definitions:

Orchestrating the sale – take charge and make sure the product gets built, tested, shipped, installed, and running, and services get implemented and followed through with. It's your responsibility to get your harvest to the market.

Acceleration – continue to maintain the partnership you created during the initial sale. Check back to monitor satisfaction and ongoing needs and other opportunities to help.

Don's To-Do List

✔ Orchestrate the sale.

✔ Accelerate the sale with push-pull activities.

✔ Get references and document return on investment.

✔ Pass on knowledge and experience to others.

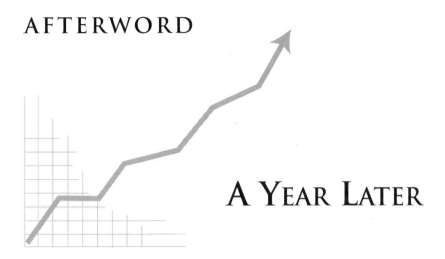

AFTERWORD

A YEAR LATER

E d sat at his desk early one morning leafing through a business magazine. Regal Electromechanical was rated as the fastest growing company in their industry, and in the top 25 overall. Ed closed the magazine and put it aside. Under it was one of the reasons for the rating – last quarter's sales results.

As Ed scanned the rows of figures, the first thing he noticed was that, for the first time in nearly three years, someone else's name was above his – Don Taylor. "Brand Don," he thought, amused. Well, this definitely called for a little teasing about the ungrateful student upstaging the kindly master.

He gathered up the results and headed down the hall.

When he reached Don's office, he stuck his head through the door.

Don wasn't there. "I'll get him later," thought Ed and headed toward the kitchen for some coffee. Along the way he heard Don's voice.

Ed paused for a moment outside the office of a saleswoman whom he knew had been struggling recently. There was Don, standing next to the familiar six-step chart talking about **Investigation** as the woman scribbled notes.

Ed moved on. It was then he realized that the student-master tease wouldn't work. There was a new **Influential Advisor** in the house.

ACKNOWLEDGEMENTS

All endeavors great or small require a foundation built on love, trust, respect and passion. I wish to acknowledge the following individuals who have made such an impact on me. Their support, guidance and hard work made this dream of *Influential Selling* possible.

First and foremost, to my brother Ned Carnes, I want to dedicate this book to you because without your incredible ability to translate complex thoughts, experiences, and concepts into real-life stories that others can read, understand, and learn from, this book would have never been possible. The impact of your talents can never truly be measured, but what you have done for me will never be forgotten. Thank you.

So many have contributed to my personal and professional success it would be impossible to acknowledge in this small space. However, without David Cottrell and his courage to stay the course, inspiration to dream big, and dedication as someone to turn to even in the darkest of my days, I would have never had the opportunity to find and live my passion … David, thank you for taking me under your wing for over 20 years now.

To my Mother and Father, James and Joyce Carnes, your support and positive influence throughout my life has set the foundation and continues to ground me on what is truly important in life. Seeing you both tackle life's joys and most difficult challenges together continues to inspire me each and every day … I love you both.

And finally to Susan, Ryan, and Morgan, you fill my life each day with such joy and meaning, God could not have blessed me with a better, more supportive family … thank you for always being there for me.

ABOUT THE AUTHOR

For over 23 years, **Ken Carnes** has developed an intense passion for both sales and leadership effectiveness. His proven successes in both areas and his ability to communicate and connect with people, has made him one of this country's most sought-after speakers and coaches. Today, Ken has the privilege of speaking to thousands of individuals during his keynotes and workshops on both sales and leadership effectiveness. In the past five years, he has personally mentored over 200 corporate executives.

Ken's first book, *Management Insights*, which he co-authored with David Cottrell, has become standard reading in many organizations for emerging high-potential employees and new managers who are building a foundation for future leadership success.

Ken's past experience includes sales, training, and senior leadership positions with Xerox, FedEx, and AchieveGlobal. Currently, Ken is a partner with CornerStone Services and is a principal with the Capital H Group, one of the fastest growing human capital consulting firms in North America today.

Ken and his wife Susan, son Ryan, daughter Morgan, and their two dogs and bird reside in The Woodlands, Texas.

Six ways to bring the *Influential Selling* message to your team:

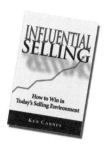

1. *Influential Selling Workshop*
   Facilitated by Ken Carnes or a certified CornerStone Services instructor, this three- or six-hour foundation-building workshop will assist every sales person, new or experienced, build a personal plan to become the Influential Advisor that top decision makers are valuing in the market today. These workshops are highly interactive and customized to your selling environment.

2. *Keynote Presentation*
   Invite author Ken Carnes to motivate and inspire your sales organization, conference, or team with the powerful message of *Influential Selling*. Each presentation is interactive, fun, and targeted to be a learning experience for you and your group.

3. *Influential Selling PowerPoint® Presentation*
   Introduce and reinforce the *Influential Selling* to your organization with this complete and cost-effective companion presentation piece. All the main concepts and ideas in the book are reinforced in this professionally produced, downloadable **PowerPoint presentation with facilitator guide and notes.** Use the presentation for kick-off meetings, training sessions, or as a follow-up development tool. **$99.95**

4. *Influential Selling* **Audio CD $19.95**

5. *Influential Selling* **Reminder Card**
   Pocket-sized, laminated. Pk/20 **$19.95**

6. *Influential Selling* **Checklist (FREE)**
   To help reinforce the concepts and provide direction on building the foundation for *Influential Selling*, please log on to www.**CornerStoneLeadership**.com and click into the *Influential Selling* section. There you will find various checklists that you can download for free. These checklists are valuable tools which can help you and your team get started on the road to becoming Influential Advisors to your prospects and customers.

Additional CornerStone Leadership Resources:

You Gotta Get in the Game ... Playing to Win in Business, Sales and Life provides direction on how to get into and win the game of life and business. **$14.95**

Monday Morning Customer Service takes you on a journey of eight lessons that demonstrate how to take care of customers so they keep coming back. **$14.95**

The Ant and the Elephant is a different kind of book for a different kind of leader! A great story that teaches that we must lead ourselves before we can expect to be an effective leader of others. **$12.95**

You and Your Network is profitable reading for those who want to learn how to develop healthy relationships with others. **$9.95**

136 Effective Presentation Tips is a powerful handbook providing 136 practical, easy-to-use tips to make every presentation a success. **$9.95**

175 Ways to Get More Done in Less Time has 175 really good suggestions that will help you get things done faster ... usually better. **$9.95**

12 Choices ... That Lead to Your Success is about success ... how to achieve it, keep it, and enjoy it ... by making better choices. **$14.95**

Orchestrating Attitude: Getting the Best from Yourself and Others by Lee J. Colan, translates the incomprehensible into the actionable. It cuts through the clutter to deliver inspiration and application so you can orchestrate your attitude ... and your success. **$9.95**

Goal Setting for Results addresses the fundamentals of setting and achieving your goal of moving yourself and your organization from where you are, to where you want (and need) to be! **$9.95**

Becoming the Obvious Choice is a roadmap showing employees how they can maintain their motivation, develop their hidden talents, and become the best. **$9.95**

Visit www.**CornerStoneLeadership**.com for
additional books and resources.

✓ YES! Please send me extra copies of *Influential Selling!*
1-30 copies $14.95   31-100 copies $13.95   100+ copies $12.95

Influential Selling   _____ copies X _____   = $ _____

Additional Leadership Development Resources

You Gotta Get in the Game	_____ copies X $14.95	= $ _____
Monday Morning Customer Service	_____ copies X $14.95	= $ _____
The Ant and the Elephant	_____ copies X $12.95	= $ _____
You and Your Network	_____ copies X $9.95	= $ _____
136 Effective Presentation Tips	_____ copies X $9.95	= $ _____
175 Ways to Get More Done in Less Time	_____ copies X $9.95	= $ _____
12 Choices …That Lead to Your Success	_____ copies X $14.95	= $ _____
Orchestrating Attitude	_____ copies X $9.95	= $ _____
Goal Setting for Results	_____ copies X $9.95	= $ _____
Becoming the Obvious Choice	_____ copies X $9.95	= $ _____
CornerStone Sales Professional Package	_____ packs X $119.95	= $ _____

(Includes all 11 items listed above)

Shipping & Handling $ _____

Subtotal $ _____

Sales Tax (8.25% – TX Only) $ _____

Total (U.S. Dollars Only) $ _____

Shipping and Handling Charges

Total $ Amount	Up to $49	$50-$99	$100-$249	$250-$1199	$1200-$2999	$3000+
Charge	$6	$9	$16	$30	$80	$125

Name _____ Job Title _____

Organization _____ Phone _____

Shipping Address _____ Fax _____

Billing Address _____ Email _____

City _____ State _____ ZIP _____

❏ Please invoice (Orders over $200) Purchase Order Number (if applicable) _____

Charge Your Order: ❏ MasterCard   ❏ Visa   ❏ American Express

Credit Card Number _____ Exp. Date _____

Signature _____

❏ Check Enclosed (Payable to: CornerStone Leadership)

Fax	**Mail**	**Phone**
972.274.2884	P.O. Box 764087	888.789.5323
	Dallas, TX 75376	

www.**CornerStoneLeadership**.com

CornerStone
Leadership Institute